Order this book online at www.trafford.com
or email orders@trafford.com

Most Trafford titles are also available at major online book retailers.

© Copyright 2009 Paul Mondor.

All rights reserved. No part of this publication may be reproduced, stored in a retrieval system, or transmitted, in any form or by any means, electronic, mechanical, photocopying, recording, or otherwise, without the written prior permission of the author.

Note for Librarians: A cataloguing record for this book is available from Library and Archives Canada at www.collectionscanada.ca/amicus/index-e.html

Printed in Victoria, BC, Canada.

ISBN: 978-1-4269-0268-0 (sc)
ISBN: 978-1-4269-0269-7 (hc)
ISBN: 978-1-4269-0270-3 (eBook)

Our mission is to efficiently provide the world's finest, most comprehensive book publishing service, enabling every author to experience success. To find out how to publish your book, your way, and have it available worldwide, visit us online at www.trafford.com

Trafford rev. 08/11/09

 www.trafford.com

North America & international
toll-free: 1 888 232 4444 (USA & Canada)
phone: 250 383 6864 ♦ fax: 812 355 4082

To thanks Dean & Dianne!

Thank you

12/19/09

Paul [signature]

I dedicate this book to living

I wrote this book just like my last one. Based on actual notes I took during the trip. These notes were put on paper exactly as I thought them. Quickly, and with the French Canadian language flowing through my mind!
This is why you will see plenty of times, phrases constructed backwards. Some other times you will read words that might be absolutely alien to you. Hey! Sometimes they are to me too!
Once I came back and decided to write about our trip, all I had to do was to expend the notes. As I read my condensed notes, details came back to me and I wrote them down! The details that is!

There are some expressions that are from the motorcycle world, some others from "Jouale"; which is the Slang I speak; and others I have no freaking clue where they came from.
I inserted some of blurbs of these notes. Some of them are in French, some others are in English and some are in God knows what!

I hope that reading this will bring you back to these days we spent together riding. I know I still laugh, and sometimes cringe reading them.
I would love to do another trip like this. But I will not! And I know you will understand why once you read me. These following words and thoughts are from my mind to yours, from my heart to yours and they are filled with all that I am!

I hope you enjoy reading them as much as I enjoyed writing them

Iceman

You will also see Harry's notes.

Notes that he took from the time he heard about my trips to the ones he took while he was on the road with me. His notes were inserted as they were written. No changes were made and I didn't correct anything.

His notes reflect who he is and how he thinks. His career as a forensic investigator with the RCMP, for 33 years has taught him a thing or two. The leg of the trip from Victoria BC to Brandon Manitoba wouldn't have been the same without Harry. Not only did we as friends experience something few do, but we also grew as well.

I learned from him and he from me. What was wild is that it gave me the chance to see with my own eyes what others saw when I made my trip in 2007. It was wild to se Harry go through what he went through.

I also saw how dangerous and yet fun the whole thing can be just by looking at him go through his days.

Would I do it again? Would I do it again with Harry?

I will answer what Harry answered.

Why not?

Enjoy

I am looking at this today and I can see that I could not quite grasp the seriousness of what I was about to embark on! I guess my 2 brain cells were not quite awake the day I decided to go on this trip. Dad used you to tell me "Paul! Think Dammit! Think!" This was a time where he would have told me so. But I am also happy I did not think too much. Otherwise I would have never made it, and I would not know what Labrador truly is like in winter on a motorcycle. A place of beauty where isolation, extreme temperatures and the vastness can either be your friends or your executioners!

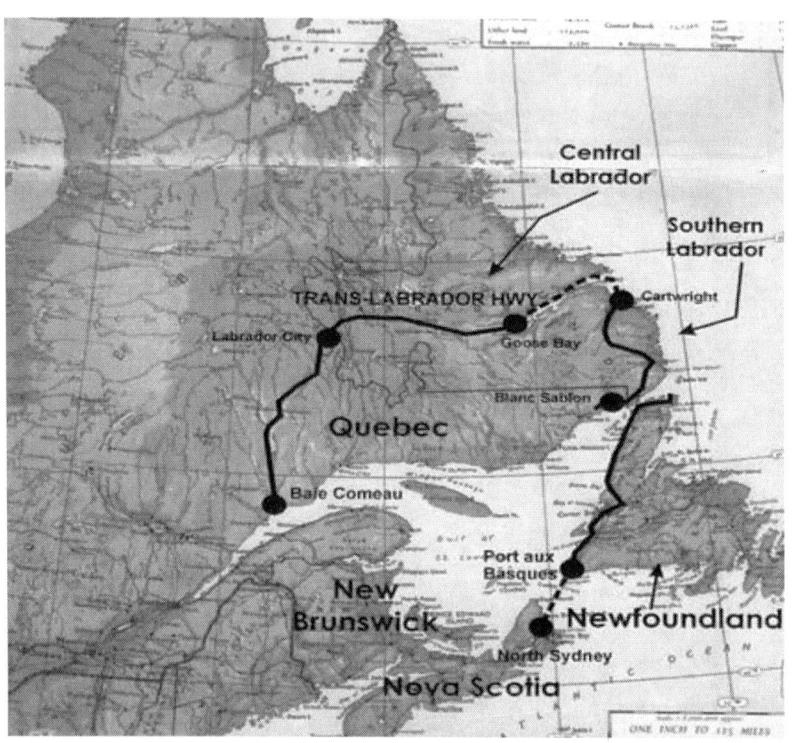

This was my eastern destination

Here we go

Table of content

Maps	*Page 7*
Harry's note	*Page 9*
Iceman 2.0	*Page 13*
Equipment	*page 23*
First day on the road	*Page 33*
Day 2	*Page 50*
Day 3	*Page 69*
Day 4	*Page 87*
Day 5,6	*Page 94*
Day 7	*Page 101*
Day 8	*Page 116*
Day 9	*Page 128*
Day 10	*Page 138*
Day 11to 13	*Page 142*
Day 14	*Page 150*
Day 15	*Page 165*

Table of content

Day 16	*Page 173*
Day 17	*Page 189*
Day 18	*Page 213*
Day 19	*Page 226*
Day 20	*Page 253*
Day 21	*Page 256*
Day 22	*Page 268*
Day 23	*Page 273*
Prologue	*Page 295*
Acknowledgements	*Page 296*
Glossary	*Page 299*

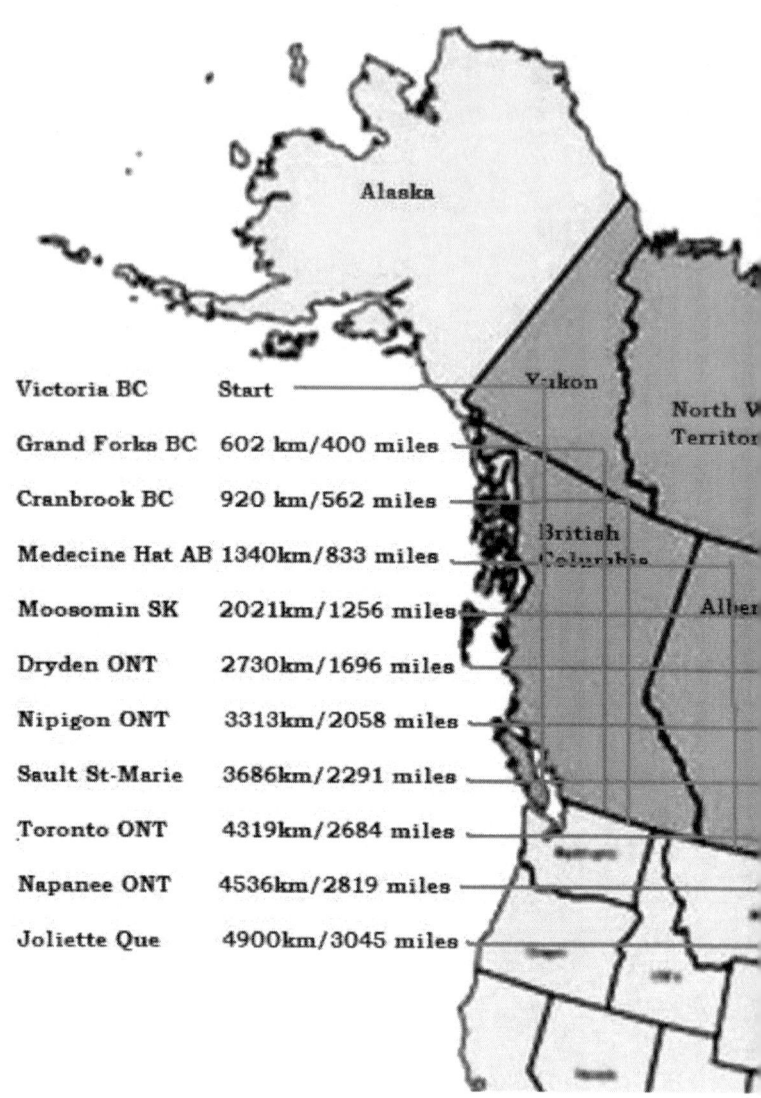

Victoria BC	Start
Grand Forks BC	602 km/400 miles
Cranbrook BC	920 km/562 miles
Medecine Hat AB	1340km/833 miles
Moosomin SK	2021km/1256 miles
Dryden ONT	2730km/1696 miles
Nipigon ONT	3313km/2058 miles
Sault St-Marie	3686km/2291 miles
Toronto ONT	4319km/2684 miles
Napanee ONT	4536km/2819 miles
Joliette Que	4900km/3045 miles

Distance/time map

Distance/time map

Harry' notes

January 11, 2007

I went to the BMW dealer and picked up my part. I got the website of Paul Mondor who is riding across Canada on a motorcycle like mine. His is a 2007, mine is a 2005. He left January 1st from here. He is now in Joliette Quebec. I am not the only crazy rider out there.

I would have like to make the trip with him but I don't know if I have enough experience. I heard about it too late in January.

January 12, 2007

I wonder if I would have gone with Paul if I had known about it earlier and had time to prepare.

February 3, 2007

I went to the BMW shop. Paul was working. I congratulated him on his trip and shook his hand. We talked some. (First time I met Paul)

November 3, 2007

I went to the BMW dealer for a light bulb and bike wash stuff. Paul was working. I talked with him. He is planning to ride his motorcycle to Goose Bay Labrador and back this winter. He has a sidecar ordered for his Dakar. He wants to extra space to carry survival gear.

Back up a bit

First I had made the comment I would have been tempted to go with him last year but I didn't know about his trip until after he was gone

That's when he told me about his plan and I could come along as I know about this one plenty early. I had to quickly back track a bit.

He continued his story. The sidecar is made in Russia and he is getting it through a dealer in Washington. He plans to have to do some winter camping along the way. I went to Terri's (my sister) in Goldstream for tea; I got to thinking about this bike ride. I have the bike, I have the tent, I have the time, my winter boots are in Manitoba but marks Wearhouse has some, Canadian Tire has the North 49 arctic suit.

I have the mitts, the electric vest, I have the sleeping bag. Paul is French and from Quebec on he would take care of us there. It would be a grand adventure. Paul invited me to come along which is quite an honour. I could freeze my ass off amongst others parts

November 4, 2007

I am still contemplating freezing my ass off across Canada with Paul. It would be quite an experience.

November 7, 2007

I just rode over to SM Cycle, Paul wasn't working today. I asked Brian Mc Dougall if anyone was going with Paul on this ride and he said no. I asked about all the other people online that said they would go with him this time and Brian said that there was about 9 hard core people that said they would and they all quit.

The last one to quit was in August. So no one is planning to go with him this winter!

So maybe Harry should go!

Could only die! They say what doesn't kill you makes you stronger. Do I want to go out and freeze my ass and other parts off? How do I train for that? I guess I could go out and ride my motorcycle naked to get used to the cold. Yu only live once apparently.

November 10, 2007

I went to the dealer and asked Paul about the trip again. He said I wouldn't have to do the whole, just whatever I was comfortable with. He would like the company a day or two or ten. He said "Make no mistake about this-it will be the toughest ride you will ever be on"

So I went home and thought about it and came up with this. I'll set my goal to get to Boissevain Manitoba. That is about 3000 kilometres; if that is enough for me I can store my bike in my plane hangar and catch the bus to Victoria. I would have to buy knobby tires for the trip and use them to go to Yellowknife or the Yukon in the spring. So I think I'll start preparing for a ride to Boissevain.

November 12, 2007

I called Paul. He is suffering with a cold! I told him of my plan to ride with him to Brandon Manitoba right up from Boissevain and decide if I'd go further after this. He thought it was a good plan.

NOTE: Paul helped me get 'Jane" my 2005 BM Dakar fitted out for the ride. I built a Lexan fairing/shield to protect my engine and my feet. I am not online so I was not aware of the ride Paul was planning. I live in Boissevain Manitoba when not on the road on my Dakar. I arrived in Victoria on October 31, 2007 with my truck and my old Airstream trailer to spend the winter in an RV Park. My motorcycle was in the back of the truck so I could ride while I was there.

Iceman 2.0
How the hell did it happen?

It has been a month since I came back from my coast-to-coast Winter Trip that took me to Cape Spear Newfoundland. I have readjusted to life at home. Frosty is tucked in the garage all cleaned up; and looking at her you would never know that she and I went through what we did. She looks like the new bike she is supposed to look like. As for me; I cannot quite say the same.

I have lost some weight, both physically and emotionally! This trip has taken only around thirty days, but it has changed me forever. I know things about myself now that I did not know before, and I also have accumulated memories and experiences that will last a lifetime.

But most importantly, I have friends now I did not have before this adventure. Their friendship will also last a lifetime. Anybody who has travelled all over or anywhere knows that when it is all said and done, the people we met along the way are what stick to our mind the most. A little bit over a year ago, Canada was a country I had crossed many times, and it has always been to me, the most beautiful country in the world. Many who have crossed its magnificent landscape know this. But now it is more than this. It left a whole new imprint on my mind. An imprint filled with the very people who have made this last trip what it is; the trip of a lifetime; Again!

From coast to coast, their faces are as unique as every mile travelled through its landscape. From the BC Logger or small town coffee shop operator to the Newfoundland fisherman or trapper, they all share one

thing in common. They have all come across my path and made the memories unmistakably personal. I can just humbly hope that I have as a motorcyclist, left an imprint on theirs.
One would think that one thing or person would stand out as THE MOST memorable one; but no!!! They all are part of this album of pictures, sounds, feelings, smells and senses that this trip has become.
I could try to sum it all up by saying what 68 newspapers, 4 National TV stations, 5 radio stations, 928 calls on my Cell phone, 487 people who have made their home available (And countless others) 8000 kilometres, 1000's of smiles and laughter, countless coffees and meals with newfound friends, 100's of websites that adopted me and 100's of thousands of people who followed me have said, but I will not! Because it is so much more than that!

I am at home now, and with all these memories flooding my mind, two words are sounding louder than ever. Two words that showed up right after I got here. They should not really be in there after all I went through, but they keep coming to me like the rhythm of a drum in a military march. Two words which are engraving themselves deeper and deeper in the back of my sometimes crazy mind. **WHERE NEXT???**

Yep! "Where next!" Absolutely brilliant! The only thing I should be thinking about now is recuperate and get back to a life of normalcy. Mind you, I have always believed that **"Normal"** is nothing but a cycle on a dryer and move on. But Noooh! Now these words and the possibilities they represent are haunting me.
I can thank Geoff in St-John's Newfoundland for this. I know he meant it, and I knew I liked the sound of it when he said it; I just did not know how much then!
Today I walked by the World Atlas in our dining room, and I tried to ignore it but I failed miserably.
As miserably as a man walking toward a woman with large boobs! He knows it is coming! He knows he cannot and should not stare; and more than ever because he is

with is partner. This fact alone should deter him from staring...

But NOOOOO! This little voice resonates in his mind. It is the voice of reason and logic. But he cannot hear it. It is soft and yet strong; but it is overpowered by every cell in his brain ganging up together against it. He is helpless and he knows it!

Alpha Sierra Sierra 1!
Bogie at 12 O'clock!
Hellfire missile loaded! Target acquired and locked on!
Standby for staring procedure!
On my mark- 3-2-1 stare! I repeat! Stare!"
Alpha Sierra Sierra 1! (ASS 1)
Staring confirmed!
Mission accomplished and all hope of a pleasant diner has been eliminated!
I repeat! Eliminated!"

At the same time the little "I told you so" Angel pops on your shoulder, and in your mind you hear what you have heard too many freaking times.

"Mayday! Mayday!
I have been hit! I repeat I have been hit!
It was a trap! I repeat it was a trap!
Enemy had engaged mind reading device and targeted our non-hostile intentions.
Has also deployed decoy and zeroed in on our location.
Confirm tonight's tactical change in sleeping location protocol!
From bedroom to couch!
I repeat "To couch!"
Enemy has me locked on and will fire unless we lay down our weapons and surrender to the idea that no matter what! WE ARE WRONG!
I repeat! Admittance of wrong is imperative!
Commence begging sequence! I repeat! Commence begging sequence!

Further instructions will follow!
Damage control protocol initiated.
Stand by for further directives!

I am looking back at the Labrador map today and I can see that I could not quite grasp yet, the seriousness of what I was about to embark on! I guess my two brain cells were not quite awake the day I decided to go on this trip.

I said it many times. Dad used to tell me *"Paul? Think Dammit! Think!"* This is a time where he would have told me so. But it is also a time where I am happy I did not! (Think) Otherwise I would have never made it and would not know what Labrador really is. A place of beauty where isolation and vastness can either be your friends or your executioners. Looking at the atlas I said to myself; *"Damn Paul you are just back and you are already thinking of the next trip! "What s wrong with you? Why are you doing this?"* I didn't know the answer to this question yet. *Unfortunately I wouldn't till I came come back from this trek!*

| **March 1st 2007** |
| *Shit! What am I thinking?* |
| *Tabarnac! Es-tu malade?* |

The next year will be spent preparing for this trip. More than a few challenges will pop during planning. Challenges that made me say *"Shit! That is serious stuff!"*

The first one!

As I did some research about Labrador, I quickly realized that this would not be remotely the same than last year's. Crossing from Victoria to Baie-Comeau where I will embark on the Trans-Labrador highway would be kind of the same.

Six thousands kilometres of wintry road conditions! But at that time of the year the TLH would be a killer. It will transform itself into a reality that I had not planned for.

"I will get back to this later!"

The second

The equipment I would need to transport with me would be totally different. As I realized what kind of weather Labrador could and would throw at me, it became pretty freaking obvious that due to the distance between inhabited points, I would need some survival equipment just in case I got stranded. Anything from food to communications systems!

The third

My motorcycle would have to be prepared totally differently. Last year was hard on Frosty, but I could always count on surrounding towns and people along the way; and being totally stranded was highly unlikely. Getting hurt was a strong possibility, but at least there were people almost everywhere.
Looking at the map of Labrador, it was obvious this was not going to be the case, and that I would need quite a bit of stuff.
I did some more research and got advice from people all over the place including Dave Barr. Dave was the first person to go across the frozen land of Russia in winter on a motorcycle! And not only that; Dave is a two leg amputee! You want hardcore? Meet Dave!
You can find about this extraordinary man on his website at http://WWW.Davebarr.com/
Dave gave me some priceless advice on what to do and what not to do in winter on a motorcycle. Advice on anything from camping, survival equipment; to weapons and maintenance! Thanks Dave! You Da Man!!!

It was also very obvious that I could not carry it on Frosty without some kind of assistance. Choices were limited. Sidecar, trailer and that was it! I am not a trailer fan, and I am sure not a sidecar fan. I had a very limited experience with trailers and none with a sidecar.

Unless you consider riding a sidecar rig for about five minutes an 'experience'. Other issues were also popping up all over the place. My original intention was to go from Baie-Comeau to Goose Bay and then catch the ferry from Goose Bay to Cartwright.
Then ride to Blanc Sablons Quebec where I could hop on the ferry to Pointe Barbe Newfoundland. Then I could ride on the Rock to Port Aux Basques, and take the ferry off the Rock to North Sidney Nova Scotia. Sounds pretty nice! Right? B-U-T! Yep! There is always many "but" within the first months of planning.
I found out that due to the ice run, icebergs and all the good stuff that Northern Labrador's winters are known for; that the ferry closes any time from early November; to late December, and reopens in the spring...
After talking with many people on the Rock and Labrador, and trying to find out if I could fly Frosty between these points; I was told that it is almost impossible and that even if I could find someone who could do it; the cost would be astronomical. Last time I checked I had no relation to Donald Trump; and Bill Gates never returned my calls. Bastard!

Meanwhile my post was gathering some attention and also attracting all sorts of naysayers. By then those who know me could tell for sure that it was only fuelling me. So I discarded them very quickly. Especially one here in Victoria that has the nasty reputation to be pretty much- everyone's pain in the ass! It would be unfair for me to name him but let's just say....Naahh!
Two months later Ural USA and I made contact. They were interested in supplying a rig for me. They wanted me to do the trip on a new Gear up two-wheel drive rig and post about it on AdvRider.com.

Actual Notes and comments from people on ADVRider.com

"And I don't know where you from but I think that's a little stupid idea..."

"Traveling the Trans lab in winter like that is unnecessarily risky. If you're lucky you may get decent weather and make it"

And the all time best

"Riding a new motorcycle with all the latest high tech gear to stay warm and alive in the middle of winter is not an 'adventure'. It has been done before. To both the North and South Poles.
If you want 'Adventure' why don't you volunteer to work in an AIDS orphanage in Africa or a Refugee camp on the Indo/Afghan border? That, to me, is an 'Adventure'"

An then you had the positive ones

"Let the naysayers shove it. Paul is not my "hero"; he's just a guy doing something adventurous.

I have been a BMW fan for years, and last year doing it on my faithful Dakar AKA Frosty turned out to be the best choice I could have made.
Now keep in mind that I had not accepted any sponsorship and was not interested in it; so doing it on an Ural was just a matter of agreeing to it. Which I did!

By this time Norm Wells, President of BMW Motorrad Canada who had been behind me on last year's trip as far as support was concerned had also told me, this time, way in advance, that if I needed anything to just ask and that they (BMW) would be in all the way.
Last year's trip benefited them in a huge way, publicity-wise speaking. And it cost them nothing! Free's good! *Hey I am not cheap! I am negotiable! I am digressing here! Aren't I!*
They recognised the attention they got and wanted to be part of this one too. May came along and the ball was rolling fast. I was in constant contact with Ural and they were keen to start. They were saying that I should get the rig by early October or late November. And that was ok with me.
I only needed a couple of weeks to do my shakedown runs. Ural enthusiasts were looking forward to see how it would fare, and others were telling me it was a bad idea, and that it would not survive. At this point even though Ural had come a long way; they still were well known to have a few issues. One of them, and not the least, was/is their reliability. It was the most important one to me.
I did not care about dealer support or anything else! I needed to know and trust that my bike would make it. The more I was hearing about it the more I was unsure. But I had committed myself to them and I did not want to go back on my word. Me and my big freaking mouth!

Summer came along, and by then I had already accumulated gear. My suit, boots and gloves were easy to choose. I would use what I had used last year because I knew it worked. My North 49 Arctic suit, my Sorel Alpha Trak boots and my BMW winter gloves supported by the Hypo Hands worked. (See my first book) But I knew that my Schuberth would not cut it. Not because it is not a good helmet, but because it does not have the air management system required to handle temperatures in the –40's to –60's that were known to happen in Labrador.

At that point I was starting to look again at the Bombardier BS2V snowmobile helmet. I had heard a lot of good things about it and after hearing from many peoples' testimonies I decided to give it a chance. I ordered it, but I needed to find out more about the options, dealer support and spare parts availability. Now the biggest problem was to find out what kind of camping equipment. IE: tent, sleeping bags, tarps, heaters, lights and fuel types I would need.

I contacted many of my friends who are still in the army and asked them to do their home work and let me know what they thought. I also contacted many manufacturers and asked them to supply me with information and test results they might have available for me on what is best and what to avoid. When they found out what it was for, some jumped in and helped me and others just basically said they could not help me. Fair enough!

One of them said *"Well! I think you are nuts but I want to help you even if it is just to be able to say we were part of this crazy adventure!"* I also asked a couple friends of mine who are in the Police and who also have been in the service for their help. At first, the idea of using propane was quickly discarded because of its low freezing point. It turns into gel at about –40C. This might not be good!

Kerosene was also discarded! Not because of its capabilities as it is a lot better than propane in cold environments; but because the heaters needed to use it are HUGE! And I did not have the room or the desire to use something this big.

White fuels like MSR were also discarded because of the reliability. I was told that they need servicing often and that they clog the burners too often. The last thing I

needed was to be stopped somewhere because I am freezing and also cussing at the heater because it will not start.
Frozen fingers and body parts mixed with a French Canadian temper, and my ability to swear in French would produce something that would probably scare the wild life right out of Labrador/Newfoundland.

I could see the wolves and caribou saying;
"Shit Man! Let's get out of here! This guy scares the shit out of me and he doesn't even have a gun!"

Many opinions later; I opted for propane, propane heaters and lights. The summer months were spent fine-tuning the rest of my equipment like tools and food.
My toolkit would be different from the extensive set I already have. I wasn't sure what I needed for the Ural but if the opinions of owners were any indication I would need a few, and quite a few spare parts.

Madina at Ural USA assured me that the Russian Factory Mechanic named Sergue would make a few modifications to insure that most of the rig would be prepped for this. They also wanted me to go see them in Seattle to work with them.
They wanted me to share my experiences in extreme winter riding with them so they could make the modifications accordingly. This would be a good chance to learn for all parties involved! *But I have to be honest!*

At that point I was still not sure about the Ural and I was constantly tempted to fall back on my other plan. My faithful Frosty! Which I knew would make it. The more I read about the Ural the more I was convinced it would fail. I often thought "Well I guess we will have to wait and see! And if it fails I will just have to come back home blame the failure on it, set up Frosty and try again!"!

List of what I carried

Stuff and tools

6 containers of propane (Small portable ones)
Coleman Ceramic heater
Complete tool kit
Car jack to lift car and bike for chain maintenance
Collapsible shovel
18 Volt rechargeable drill with charger
25 feet extension cord
Jumping cables
Ground tarp (For under tent)
Candles (you can heat a tent buried in snow in 10 minutes)
Complete first aid kit
Spare tubes, plugs, filters and levers
Spare light bulbs (Lots of them)
Matches and butane lighter.

Knife and axe
Plenty of lube ad rust inhibitor
Grease gun
Flashlight
One 8 gallon jerry can of fuel (Ballast as well)
One 2 gallon can of fuel (Outside rig)
1 can of ether (Be surprised what you can do with this)
2 litres of oil
I can of chain lube (Amsoil MP) this shit is the best!
1 can of electric contact cleaner
1 big can of Whoopass!
1 really big can of cohunes protective lotion

Camping equipment

Base camp sleeping bag
Spare paper filter for my face mask (Not enough, see later)
Spare gloves
North 49 arctic suit
Sorel Alpha Trak boots
Hypo Handz
Aerostich Darien suit (Switched to North 49 suit at -40C)
BMW Santiago boots

Food

4 dozens of hi potency protein bars
Concentrated cayenne pepper powder
Water bottle (Don't ask)
Granola and fruits
Vitamins and supplements
Gum
1 bag of dried meat

Electronic equipment

Sony® 80G DVD video camera
Sony® Digital SLR
Minolta®300mm AP4 Telephoto lens
Spot® personal GPS tracker
HD tripod
Sport shots helmet mounted camera
Cell phone
Satellite phone (From 2 Seasons hotel in Labrador City)

That would make the failure easier to digest! Right? No freaking way! It would have downright pissed me off!

Fall was approaching and things were moving along fine. I was working at SM Cycle at that point and I intended to work there till the end of November when I would need to focus only on my trip. Customers and friends were coming in the shop and they were also getting excited.
This allowed me to see that the reaction they had about the trip was different from last year. I was starting to see and feel a lot more fear and worries in their eyes and words.
They all seemed to agree that the trip from here (Victoria) to Baie-Comeau would be just like last year and that the real challenge would be the TLH. A lot of them had done their homework and already knew how dangerous it could be and that I should reconsider. They were saying that the extreme temperatures mixed with isolation would be too much to handle, and that combined; they increased the risk immensely. I tried to justify my confidence but I could not! I guess they knew me by now and knew that only I would be able to change my own mind; and that hearing all this was only, for some unknown reason, fuelling me even more.
After a while I contacted a friend of mine who had been attached with the SAR techs in Goose Bay for many years and shared my plan with him. This guy has known me since high school and we were raised in the same neighbourhood; and we also have the same raw appetite for life.
He said "Paul! *I know there is no point in me wasting my breath telling you this is the wildest thing I have ever heard being planned around these parts; and I have rescued some pretty crazy people here! So I will not try! But you have to know this. In this area, at the time you will travel through it, the weather is nasty enough and the conditions whether they are road conditions or flying conditions are bad enough that we are unable to attempt rescue sorties 60% of the time or more. Do-you-hear-me? The risks are high enough that even we; will not venture*

out there! Your call my friend! Here is my Sat phone number! Use it if needed! But Paul! Make me a promise! Promise me you will get a GPS personal tracker or at least sign off one of the free ones in Labrador that you can return once you are out of this white hell safe and sound! Meanwhile I will let the guys around here know that you will be on the TLH at that time of the year, and that if a call comes in and we can go out, we will not waste time trying to find out whether it is a prank call or not! We will know it is you! Good luck Paul!"

This alone should have been a sobering enough call! But nope!! Not to yours truly! Looking back, it is pretty damn obvious I was laughing at the strong dose of reality I was being given before I left. I guess the lesson I learned on my 2007 trip was great but not great enough! I had found myself and I wanted more! Don't ask? I have always said that if something is meant to happen; it will happen no matter what. "No amount of worrying will prevent what is meant to happen from happening!"

September rolled in as fast as a politician runs out of seminar about integrity and honesty!
One day while I was working at the BMW shop, a customer of mine, and soon to be one of my best friend (I just didn't know it yet) walks in the shop. His name is Harry Harding. A retired RCMP forensic CSI!!
33 years of it have made him a man with a very interesting view of life. A view that allows him to look at it from a very different point of view! I am sure that after seeing blood, gore and body parts for this long and reconstructing the events that led to shit like this; you end up looking at life differently than most people! In-Freaking-Deed!! I am sure that Harry grabs life by the horns and that he would not have it any other way. So here he is, as tall as life; walking to the counter to order parts for his 2005 Dakar! Then he walks to me and tells me that he has just come back to Victoria from Southern Manitoba to spend winter here. He has bought a house in Boissevain Manitoba and wants to ask me if I would consider the idea of him joining me on the trip.

He reminds that when I came back last year he and I had chatted, and he had asked me to let him know if I were to do something like this again. He looks at me and says 'Well I am here! You need a partner?"

Harry is 6 foot 3 with salt and pepper hair tied up in pony tail, and a long beard covering his face. He wears his glasses on the tip of his nose, and behind them, are eyes twinkling with a child-like eagerness to be out there playing. His smile says "I am real!" I said *"Sure!" let's get together and discuss this. You might change your mind when you see what it takes and how horribly wrong it could go!"*

Harry Harding

I didn't not want to sugar coat it because I already knew that the TLH would make last year's trip look like child's play. The least I could do was be honest with him; and if he still chooses to come, it will be because he knows he can do it. Over the next few weeks we will get together many times. These get together were pretty straight forward. He asked me questions about what I thought he would need for this trip, and he went out and bought it. Suit, boots, gloves, and equipment for his bike as well as modifications for it! I gave him the Hypo hands I had on Frosty last year and also the fork covers I hand-made for her. He got the shield for the front of his engine built and gathered all the gear he needed.

Harry did not want to buy a GPS tracker because I would have one. See-Harry is a No Tech guy! His journal consists of hand written notes in notebooks that he fills up with real photos he glues onto the pages. Over the years he has accumulated 84 of these books and each has an average of 390 pages. That is a whole lot of notes. I am sure the things he has written in there about his work and his experiences would make Stephen Spielberg salivate! Before I knew it Harry had bought all his gear, had tested it, and was ready to go. I, on the other hand could not quite say the same thing. I was so far behind for a while I thought I was first!

At the beginning of October I received a call from Madina at Ural USA telling me that they have to bail out. The reason given is that the rig they wanted to give me would not be produced on time for me to leave. They also told me something about some sort of export problem they had, and that they ran into problems on how to assign this rig to me as far as registration was concerned.

To be honest with you! I never bought this story! I think they did the smart thing and bailed out instead of seeing their rig fail midway with so many people watching.

> **October 12th 2007**
>
> *Holy shit! I am so relieved I will go on Frosty! I see now that I couldn't have enjoyed the trip worrying all the time whether or not this Gear Up thing would crap out on me or not!*

I suppose they were not ready for that! I was at the shop when I got the call. I have to admit that I was relieved. I still had not gotten over the fear and doubts about the Ural's abilities to survive this. I got on my cell, phoned Norm Wells, and asked him if he was still interested in the trek. He said `Whatever you need Paul I am here!"* I told him about the sidecar idea and to make a long story short he said he would pay for it.

Like I said-*"Norm! You da Man!!"* I contacted Dauntless Motors in Enumclaw Washington. They are North America's; if not the world's biggest sidecar outfitters and their reputation is as solid as can be.

I phoned and talk to Jay, the owner of the company and told him about my plan. This guy came aboard quickly and efficiently. He was eager to help me, and wanted to make it right the first time.

I just hope he could teach me how to ride a sidecar over nine thousand kilometres of ice in his parking lot; and in half an hour! He advised me to buy a Sputnik Sidecar! Looks like no matter what; Russia would be part of this trip, whether I liked it or not! But this Russian product existed and was right there waiting for me. I had more confidence in the Sputnik than I had in the Ural!

Я имел больше доверия в Sputnik чем я имел в Ural!

Hey! There is more to me than just my good looks you know??

After working out the options and details and agreeing on a price, we arranged for me to ride Frosty to his place where she would be outfitted with her new appendage.

Enumclaw is only 2 1/2 hours from Vancouver. He would lend me a company pickup truck to commute back and forth between the motel and the shop because it would take two days to install.

I got to Enumclaw on a Monday night to be at the shop first thing Tuesday morning. They had planned to have it done by Tuesday afternoon. I have to admit that I was nervous about the whole sidecar idea. This trip would be my first experience. Talk about learning the hard way! It is like;

"Here Paul! Sit here? This is what we call an F-18 Fighter jet! Do not let it impress you! See this button? When I get off the ladder and pull it away, push it. The cockpit cover windshield thingie will come down! Look under the seat and pull out the instruction manual. Just go through it, and take off! Remember-this mission is extremely dangerous and your ability to control this plane will decide whether or not you will succeed! Ah! And survive! Oh-Yeah! Did I also mention you could die? Maybe not! Have a good flight Paul and God speed!"

This scenario does not make any sense right?? Well! Taking off with a sidecar to cross Canada and Labrador when it is the first time you drive a rig like this is as stupid. But hey! I am The Iceman and I can do it!!!!!

Ok! Where is that BC Bud roach I rolled ten minutes ago? Ah! Here it is! "UffhhssssSSHHHHHHHH! Ah! Makes more sense now Cheech!

Anyway! Where was I? Ah yes! It turns out that the mounting system was made for a 650GS, which is about two inches lower, so the lower torque arm were not long enough for the Dakar. They had to modify it by extending it. This required cutting, welding a longer tube etc. This would be done by the earliest Tuesday afternoon! I told Jay not to rush I was there and I wanted to job done right. It will be finished when it will be finished!
It was noon Wednesday when I rolled out of Dauntless Motors. The guys were awesome and the service #1. If you ever need a sidecar; this place is THE place to go. After a bit of practice in their yard-about thirty seconds of it-I took off. I did not know what the hell camber or toe-in was; but I thought I could find out soon enough!
I did in-freaking-deed!

From notes I wrote that day

Some of my first words coming onto the road were *"Holy crap Batman! What-the-hell-is-this?"*

These things ride like a snowmobile or an ATV or something! But it isn't a bike!! This is way too weird!"
Before I left, and during the days I was there, I read the sidecar bible that Jay gave me. It clearly says in there that this is not a motorcycle anymore and that any attempt at riding a sidecar rig like it will definitely result in an accident and injuries. That is if it goes well. *"You think??"*
Half a mile down the road from Dauntless, my first curve is silently waiting for me. It also knows I am riding or should I say driving a sidecar rig for the first time. It is a right hand turn. Not a bad one! The type of turn that posts a 45 MPH speed limit and that any motorcyclist riding <u>A-MOTORCYCLE</u>, motorcycle being the key

word here; would take on easily at 90 – 100 MPH without even sweating. Remember I have been riding two-wheelers for well over 1 million miles and I have ridden sidecars for...............Well? ....let's see here?????? Uhhhhhhhh!...... ZERO miles! I look at the curve and I can see the end of the apex, I am riding/driving at 45 MPH and initiate the *"start-try-begin-dream-attempt to turn-then realize that holy shit it is not turning even though I want it to turn-why is it so f^%$# hard to turn this F%$#@ handlebar-it d.....not HOOOLY SHIiiiiiIIIIT-here we go-here's the ditch"* manoeuvre; and across the oncoming traffic lane I go.

Thank God there are no cars coming. I am not turning. I am going straight for this magnificent row of 80 foot tall poplars. *"Ah great! Just f%$#@ great! Half a mile down the road and I crash! $15,000 for the bike, $4000 for the sidecar, total 19k- there is 5280 feet in a mile- half of this 2640- there are 31680 inches in this half miles- divide $19000.00 + by 31680- that is 59.74 cents an inch travelled- that is one expensive lesson you moron!"*

I am sure I was thinking something like this, except the math part as I was trying to make the damn thing turn, but I was too busy freaking out and cannot remember. I quickly remember what I had read; and I push on the left handlebar. And VOILA! The car wheel is hovering about two feet above the tarmac. Brilliant! Absolutely brilliant! But at least now I am turning. It is said that once the sidecar wheel is off the ground the rig handles like a two wheeler. Uh-You think? I don't F%$#@ think so! When I turn left on my bike-I am leaning left-not right! Why do you say it turns like a bike once the car wheel is off the ground? I will tell you why! Because there is no truth to this BS! None! Zip! Nada! Nothin! Zero! Niet! Sweet f%$#@all! Yes Sir-E! Anyway! Where was I? Oh yeah! Fighting for my life!

I make the curve or at least change trajectory enough to miss the poplars, and get back on the road. To my relief there is a gas station right there on my right, and in my

path! And with graceful out of control manoeuvring skills I keep going in my half-ass general direction and end up in the gas station's parking lot. I was about as smooth as a sumo wrestler performing the Nut Cracker ballet. There is a guy in the phone booth right bedside where the rig comes to a stop bouncing up and down in an ever going wiggling jiggling way, just like a pile of Jell-O does when it hits the ground.
He looks at me with a blank look in his eyes and keeps talking. But I know what his look was saying. It was saying "Man it makes the idea I had to marry my cousin look good!"
I get off the rig, take off my helmet, and look at the seat to make sure my sphincter has not sucked up a four square inch piece of seat material, and that shit in my underwear was not oozing out of my suit collar. I said to myself *"HMMM! That was really smart Butt head! All this happened in one minute and you have another 2 1/2 to 3 hours to go. Out of this, I-5 at rush hour for 1 1/2 hour. How the hell am I going to survive this?"* Like usual I said to myself; *"Ah shut up Paul and just f$#@ing do it!"*

It was pretty tense; but I did it. There is nothing like quality time spent on a sixty foot wide slab of concrete filled with Soy- No fat - no whip - Mocha Latte holding - I had a bad day - I am horny - I cannot make my zillion $$ mortgage payment for my too f$#@ing big house - and my 4 cars - my ex has garnished my pay cheque - shit is the price of gas ever high - look at this moron on a sidecar in late October - get the f$#@ out of my way SUV driving Washingtonian- screaming *"Please?? Do not break? Do not slow down! Do not turn!"*
If I had been a drinker, this would have sobered me up forever. I don't drink and it almost got me to start!!

End of notes

By the time I reached the ferry terminal I was going through traffic like I was on two wheels. NOT!!! Too early in the game! But at least I was alive and a better rider for it. This is me! I have always learned the hard way! I finally made it home. In one piece! Mind you I cannot quite say the same thing about the countless drivers I most likely freaked out.

**Above:
Frosty before the uglyorangectomy**

**Below:
With her new color**

Now that I was home, I could deal with my most immediate and urgent problem. The sidecar was painted at the factory in some kind of butt ugly- if I were drunk- it would make me puke- safety orange.

This had to go; otherwise drivers would be convulsing with disgust and drive me off the road just for the sake of self-preservation. I found a place in Victoria that would paint it the same color than Frosty! Hey! I have pride too. A few modifications needed to be done as well. First the shock had to go. The shock on the sidecar would bottom out just looking at it. I found a front shock for a BMW R1200RT and did a few modifications to put it on. What a difference. The whole rig handled differently. Before I put it on the whole thing would wobble like Jell-O® when I would take a turn.

Now it was well planted and felt secure in turns. Then I fitted a good dual purpose tire on it. The stock one might have been good to go shopping for Vodka on asphalt or hang around at the Starbuck's with the concrete cowboys and squids, but it would definitely not cut it on the TLH with gear in the car. Plus it looked like it belonged on a Moped or a scooter! Just kidding! A moped!! No nasty Emails please!

I removed the sidecar seat to turn it in to a cargo sidecar (It is designed for this as well), put a PIAA light in the front, a second battery, a built-in sealed relay circuit, a aluminum plate on the front corner to hold another jerry can and rigged the custom built brake lever adjacent to Frosty's rear brake pedal so I would have brakes on the sidecar wheel. The sidecar was ready, the bike was ready! Harry was ready and so was his bike. I was ready! Well almost! All I had to do on Frosty was to get the new Ohlin's shock on the rear installed. I ordered it with a custom 400 lbs spring on it. The whole thing was starting to come together. Harry was psyched and so was I. But I have to admit I was wishing others felt the same way. I had support, and people around me had confidence in my skills and ability to do things like this, but this time they did not express as much confidence in me this time. Looking back, maybe they had just surrendered to the idea that it would not change a thing and that they could support me but in silence. I read Ted Simon's book "Jupiter's travels" and at one point he writes about how he was wondering why he was doing this second trip.

Harry ready to roll

It is easy to get into a gloomy mode and admit defeat to the enemy inside; when we can't even understand why we would put ourselves through things that challenge the most basic logic and common sense. But everything happens for a reason. Ted found his answers during his hardest and most challenging times; and will carry with him this discovery for the rest of his life. He did not know why, but he knew he had to find himself and that if he went all over the place; he would eventually run into himself. And he did! Did he ever? And when he did, the man he discovered was simply the man he had become! I went through this on my 2007 trip. It was a hard lesson, but it was one that is valuable beyond words. This time the reason was escaping me! Again! I most likely would find out in the future, but I couldn't say for sure what it would be.

The two amigos ready to go

I still was trying to ignore this annoying feeling I had because many people around me did not approve of what I was about to do. Why was it suddenly so freaking important to be approved of? I never cared before! Why should I give a crap now?
What was it that had changed so much? I always said that I have lived my life ignoring my fears. Bla-Bla-Bla! It sure did not feel like it at that time!
I have become used to fight this natural fear inside me; and have developed a weapon system that gives me an edge in this battle. Or did I really bullshit myself? Could I be hungry for something?
This time though, the enemy felt different, and the weapons were not effective against it. It wasn't me I had

to fight, it was others. I kept thinking *"How the hell do I fight this?"* We'd see! So enough psycho-babble!
Everything was ready. The days were rolling by and the countdown was painfully slow. I was ready and there was still about a week to go before D- Day.

> **Note: I see now that my struggle was mainly caused my Christmas. Even though I am not as bad as I use to be; this time of the year really F%$#@s me up**

Here is an excerpt from my notes before I left.

Today I decided to change part of the plan where I was supposed to leave the island on the first ferry on the 1st of January and leave on the 2nd of January instead. This will allow me to spend the 1st with Melanie and my friends.
The Christmas holidays went by fairly quietly. Thank God! I am not a big Christmas fan! Never was! It is the hardest time of the year for me; and has been for as long as I can remember. I cannot associate joy and harmony with this time of the year. To me it is a time where hypocrisy and stress reign as kings, and raise havoc in the best of families, and in the strongest hearts and souls.
I do not know how this started or maybe I choose not to remember; but I refuse to let a date on a calendar tell me that I HAVE to give and RECEIVE. Talk about pressure. Yes! There is most likely bitterness in there somewhere; and I do not know where it is from. I could blame my divorced parents, the traumatic events I went through in my life so on and so forth Bla-Bla-Bla! But I will not! The truth is that I made a long series of choices as an adult and it has made me this way! My call!
Mind you- my Christmases are getting better as years go by. Melanie and those around me know that, and

respect my choices and who I am... Melanie and I had a great Christmas with friends and family and it never grew out of proportion or control. I didn't want the added stress to come along for the ride. Too much at stake and I wanted to have all my wit when I left.

First day of 2008 is now here; and only 24 hours to D-Day! Harry has moved his RV out of the lot, and brought it to his sister's for the winter. He had a good Holiday time as well! He is like me as far as all this is concerned. We had him over for Christmas and he thoroughly enjoyed the fact that it was small, simple and easy.
Tomorrow I have the meeting at Island View beach on where a group of the Vancouver Island BMW riders club gathers with hot drinks (No alcohol) and good cheer to ring in the New Year. Yours truly has another agenda. I am the only one who does the polar bear swim in the near freezing waters. Am I still going to be alone in the 40 degree water? I will see tomorrow!

January 1st 2008
Polar bear swim

As usual cameras were ready as I stripped down to my shorts while everybody else was bundled up in their riding suits, tuques and mittens. I walked to the beach in the howling wind, and came to a windsurfer fighting his rig in the wind all dressed up with his dry suit and hood. The contrast was funny. He quickly looked at me, looked away, and did a double take like he was saying "What the hell?" I asked him how he was doing while I am walking in the water. He didn't answer! Waves were crashing and I just kept going. When the water level got to my waist I dove in and started swimming. The cold took my breath away.

Literally! I had trouble breathing. Normally I stop on the beach and concentrate on my breathing and heart beat. But this time I did not stop. I went straight in. I am the only one of this merry bunch who does this! I still hope someone will join in one day; but I doubt it. Still love you guys! In my mind (My mind being the key words here!),there, is no better way to start a winter motorcycle trip than to jump in close to freezing water to ring in the New Year; and let Mr Cold know that he can try to take me on, but that he does not stand a chance!

Yeah right! My penis had shrunk so much that it was coming out of my ass! Man it was cold!
Afterward we all headed to Bill's house for coffee, chilli, soup and a big serving of friendly BS. Motorcyclists' favourite food! This to me is more like what the Holidays should be like. No stress, no shopping, no I have to and should haves and what not's.

I spent the rest of the day alone with Melanie. Tomorrow will come around quicker than I think!

Good night

End of notes

January 2nd 2008
First day on the road

I got up, got dressed. I kissed Melanie goodbye and gave her big hug, knowing that inside; her heart was not filled with excitement like mine was. I just didn't know yet to which point.
When I got out, Harry was there waiting in the driveway; and shortly after my friends Brian and Scott also arrived. They wanted to escort harry and I to the ferry terminal. The ride was cold, and it was raining. None of us minded that anyway. This is what January is like on Vancouver Island! At least we can ride in January. Or should I say "Most could" We stopped outside the ferry terminal where we took pictures (They all turned out like shit!), shook hands, gave hugs and we were on our way.

On the ferry to the mainland on January 2nd 20008. D-day!

Many people do not like the fact that we; as Island residents, have to take the ferry to get off the island and pay a bundle for it. And a bundle it is! Let's just say that Al Capone has nothing on the guys who run the BC

Ferries Corporation. These guys are not only crooks; they are good at it! Yes! I do not like them! You sensed that didn't you? Moving on! But nevertheless I have always like taking the boat. To me it is a time of transition. It is a time where I go from normal life to vacation mode. A whole hour and a half where I will watch the ocean go by, seagull dance over the decks in the hope someone will toss them some form of food; if you can ferry food, food! I have the habit of going to the coffee shop, get a coffee and come back down on the vehicle deck for the duration of the sailing.

There are large openings/windows where we park the motorcycles I can comfortably lean on the ledge, sip my coffee, and watch the world sail by without these camera toting-post cards writing-ugly hat wearing- map reading-car renting-garbage throwing tourists. **I remember someone once who was wearing a T-Shirt saying "Tourist season! Where do I get my license?" I loved it!** And let's not forget about the screaming kids running at warp speed by the "No running" signs on the passenger decks.

The crowds on the ferries are the only thing that annoys me. It is like they are invading my bubble, my breathing space. I do not care what they think, where they went and what they saw. This is my vacation and I do not want them to be part of it. Other motorcyclists on the boat- Sure! BUT NOT CAGERS!

That day was different though. I was embarking on something that so far looked like it would be harder than anything I have ever done (didn't I say this last year?), and I was also sharing the experience with a close friend of mine. The sailing was spent talking and laughing. Harry asked many questions. He understood what was ahead for him and me; but he also knew he could turn around any time. I was not be there to baby sit him; and same for him. It would be his skills and determination that would get him through, and nothing else. I could, and would help him by giving him advice and Lord knows I wanted him to get through this, but he knew that it was HIS ride!

Looking at his bike I was sure that the big duffle bag he has strapped on his rear seat would become a hell of a problem when we would start hitting slippery stuff. We had discussed it, but he was ok with it. He had the studs on his bike, front and rear, and had been riding with them for two weeks. But the high weight on his bike would make the bike do one thing only. Slide from underneath him. We'd deal with that later! I'm sure the people who were watching us and hearing us could sense a certain level of fear in our voices. I was trying hard to fight it, and Harry's laughter and relaxed attitude were reassuring me and also impressing the hell out of me considering what we were doing.

He was saying he was relaxed and looking forward to this; but I couldn't help but wonder how it could be. For crying out loud! He had never done winter riding before, and now; he was about to cross the Rockies and part of the prairies in winter on two wheels. Then I remembered feeling the same way last year.

Like I said before, I am sure his thirty-one year career as an RCMP CSI would come in handy. All my friends on the island without exception would not ride with me when there is even a slight chance of flurries. They are understandably stopped dead in their tracks by fear. And yet, here's Harry; just going at it like a ride in the park!

The long range weather forecast for the next week did not look good! There was already a lot more snow on the ground then there was last year when I took off. We had not decided yet which road we would take; the Trans-Canada (Route 1), or Highway 3 in southern BC. Just like I did last year, it would be a decision that would be made in Hope BC. <u>The city's name could not be more appropriate.</u> We would ask for an update and then we would either go north or east. Harry liked the idea of taking Route 3 for one reason only. I took the Trans Canada last year and it would be great if I could say that

I did both of them in the winter. It had nothing to do with him. What do you say to that? He'd follow me no matter what! So this was it. The plan called for Harry to ride with me as far as he could; and hopefully to Brandon Manitoba. Depending on how he would do, how he would feel about this winter riding stuff; and most importantly how we would be getting along.
It was after all our first ride together. Who knows! Maybe all he'd want to do would be to kill me, grind me up in a shredder by the time we reached Brandon.
"Hi officer! Paul Who? Never heard of him!"

So here we go!

Frosty and Icycle were sitting there on the car deck; the only two of their kind. I knew it would be a long time before we'd see some more of their kind.
Harry's bike was christened Icycle by my friends John and Rhea Cavelti's children. Rhea has been involved quite a bit in preparing the whole thing and her kids who know me as "The mint man" because the first time I met them at the BMW shop I gave them the whole bowl of mints; wanted Frosty to have a named partner. So Icycle it was! After spending the sailing by the bikes' side, we were finally nearing Tsawassen; I was hyper, and so was Harry. We shook each other's hand and saddled up.
People around us on the vehicle deck looked at us like we were aliens. I guess in many ways we were. I was as alien to them in this environment as people driving SUV's are to me when I see them caged in, driving on the wonderful roads that we as motorcyclists have learned to love so much.
Down went the ramp; and off we rode! I was thin-king of how I felt last year when I got off the ferry by myself and how lonely it was. This time I had Harry with me, and realized that the dynamics caused me to feel differently. Not in a bad way; just different! I had tried to figure it out many times so far, and it was hard to explain and even understand. It was not just because I was sharing my experience with a friend; it was deeper than that.

We both knew what was ahead, and that it would be extremely challenging at best. Mr Winter had sure showed his cold ugly face so far in a way that was saying "Better hold on!! I will give you a good shake!" The ride to Hope was uneventful! That was kind of expected. It was wet, grey and miserable. A typical BC winter day at its best! We stopped at the Chevron gas Station for our first break where fuel and coffee were in order.

After spending about twenty minutes, we decided to go on Hwy 3. It really came down to a flip of a coin! Plus harry still wanted us to do together something I had not done yet! As we approached Manning Park and as the elevation increased, winter started getting in our face.

Hope BC. Where we turned onto Hwy 3 East

What was grey winter scenery with trees asleep for the winter, turned into a white, slippery and unforgiving mess! But hey! That is what we were there for!

Snow was getting deeper and deeper as we climbed. Slush was covering the road; and mixed with salt, gravel and sand, quickly turned into our first high pucker factor moment. I had warned Harry to always keep an eye in his mirrors and watch for vehicles that could/would be throwing shit at us while passing. Being caught in a wave of frozen salty and sandy crap is no fun.

The same thing applied to oncoming traffic. We had to check where their wheels were tracking and brace ourselves when some idiot was driving in the thick patch and spraying us.

I had learned the hard way that the-You go where you look-principle applies to cars, trucks and everything else on the road too...

As they came towards us, we could see them looking at us as if saying "What the hell!" And as they did; their vehicles veered a bit to their left just enough for their wheels to track in this semi-solid frozen cocktail, sending a wave of debris that scared the living hell out of us! Every-single-f%$#@g-time!
The road was already scary enough without having others making it scarier.
We also had to change line constantly because we could not track where we wanted. I am sure we looked like we were waltzing most of the time.
I have gone through this last year, and I remembered my lesson well. Looking in my mirror, I noticed that Harry was also learning it as he tried to follow my line. This made it a bit easier and helped him to wiggle a bit less and dance more. By dancing I mean what the bike does on the snow when you keep the pressure off the handlebars, put your weight on the pegs and steer with your feet. The front end dances as the bike freely tracks forward. It really works well.
Less weight on the front-more on the rear-more traction- you know what I mean- right? Low CG????

Ok-moving on!

I was busy looking ahead; and believe me, it is a full time exercise in concentration. At the same time I wanted/had to keep an eye on my wing man. *Dammit! I sound like Tom Cruise! Not good!*
Somehow it feels like shit happens quicker on ice. In summer time you have time to say *"Holy shit!"* as you feel yourself going ass over tea kettle. But when it happens in winter it is like you only have time to say or think *"Holy"* and that is it! You are tobogganing down the road.
Harry was doing well. As a matter of fact he was doing pretty freaking well. As we approached the summit of Manning Park pass I pulled over in a roadside park. Because I had the hack I had fewer worries about coming to a stop; it is when I pulled over I made my first mistake. Having a sidecar has its advantages, and also it

down sides. You stay up! But when you hit deep shit, the hack pulls on you. I know! I know! I can hear the Ural guys saying "This would not happen if you had a two-wheel drive!" and they are right! Let's not start on this ok? My mistake is I should have slowed down before pulling over. As I pulled over all I had to worry about was this, but Harry followed me; and not being used to it, he hit the brakes and down he went. Slow speed, no damage, but down! I walked back to him and helped him get Icycle up. He looked at me and said with a huge grin on his face "*My first one! Good! This was the hardest! Getting passed my first fall! I am passed this now!*" I knew right there and then we would be ok! No stress! Not even a worry! Just a grin! He wasn't even showing regrets that he had embarked on this trip or madness with me. We took a few pictures and talked a bit as traffic went by. Later in the trip I found out that a friend of mine; Kootenay Kid was driving in that area and wrote about it on the blog later on.

Harry in Manning Park

Riding a motorcycle in winter in the biggest country in the world, "I know! I know! Russia!" and I come across someone I know. I love Canada!! A bit later down the road we stopped at Manning Park Lodge to hit the can and take the scenery in. But in winter the crowd in there is different. No RV driving-map reading- straw hat wearing tourist around.

Quote: *"Hey Paul, my wife and I passed you guys on the highway just East of Manning Park. She wouldn't believe I knew who you were. I have to say it was quite a sight to see from the safety of my truck. The next day my brother called me in Duncan to tell me he had seen a crazy man on a motorcycle in Castlegar at the Chevron. When I told him your story he was in awe and concerned about the weather. But you will push on and prevail I told him, so please do just that Paul, push on and be safe. I figure if you made it thru the Kootenays in the winter while it was snowing you should be ok for a while. Take care and have fun."*

Hwy 3 is not that popular in winter. It is used by people who can drive in bad conditions, and by people who HAVE to. A few people approached us to take pictures. And after asking the customary 'why' and 'where' they walked away with a funny look on their faces when we answered "Labrador". Most likely worried that this craziness we are afflicted with might be contagious.

I tried to reassure some people, and let them know that it was all perfectly safe, but for some reason I was having problems convincing them. Go figure! Like I told them; craziness is relative! What is crazy for one is normal for another. Depending which side of the asylum's fence you're standing on; riding a motorcycle in winter in Canada is absolutely normal.
We also tried to make them understand that cold on a bike is the same as cold on a snowmobile, but this got us nowhere. I guess it was another of these things that if you have to explain it; they won't understand it!
And if Harry takes his helmet off when I try to explain things: all hope is lost. Long beard decorated with icicles! Pony tail with ice dangling at the end, and a six foot three frame in a salt covered suit will apparently make one stop asking questions.
I guess he has this look that might make someone wonder whether or not he should be out there lose in

the world, where there are children and women. Don't be afraid people? The man has spent 33 years as an RCMP CSI for crissesake! If you are afraid of him, you should be afraid of everyone. *"But who the hell is this guy with the funny accent?"*
AHHHHH! The hell with them! As the trip progressed we'd make our own new friends. We will spend a lot of times with, **stupor**, the **holy shit family**; the **what the hell** gang and the **it seemed like a good idea at the time** society. I know! I know! We should always put our best behaviour on! But to be honest with you, I have not gotten where I am at 47 with a Boo Hoo-I am scared of what people will think of me-attitude! And judging by Harry's look; I think he has come to believe the same thing too.
Anyway! We ended up making it to Grand Forks. It was wild at times, but we made it.

Rest Area outside Osoyoos BC

Grand Forks felt like it was a nice place to call home for the night. Plus it was already dark out there and this area is not a good place to ride at night in summer. Never mind in winter! And we were bagged! We had a

great day and we were both pretty happy about how it went. While I was unpacking and going through my routine, Harry went to the store and picked up some snacks and drinks. (Beer)
We spent an hour or so chatting about what had happened in the day and what we learned.
As I listened to him talking and laugh, I knew I had made the right choice when I agreed for him to join me.

I know a lot people who ride. A lot of them are extremely good riders. But of all the people I know; Harry is the only one I would trust to share all this with. *This was no easy shit!*
This trip would not only test us as men; (My friend Dave Wells calls me "Girl") but would also test our friendship, and our ability to ride together.

Laughing my ass off that night in Grand Forks BC after a good day spent on our motorcycles, fighting the snow and the cold, I knew we would pass the test with flying colours

Good night.

Harry's notes

January 2, 2008

It took me a while to fall asleep last night. I wake up at 12:30 Am and again at 4:00 AM. My alarm went off at 4:35 AM. My mom made me tea and toasts and loaded my bike and was off around 5:30 Am and at Paul's at 5:45AM.

It was wet and snowy through Manning Park, Paul pulled over off in the snow to see how I was doing, I pulled over in the snow 4-6 inch of it and started to slip as I slowed down and then my bike fell over and me too but I wasn't under the bike. Paul came over and helped me get my bike up. No damage to me or the bike.

Day2

Grand Forks BC, January 3rd 2008
Up at 7:00 and left by 8:00

Grand Forks BC in the morning
A cool -15C

The roads in Grand Forks were slick with packed snow. The start was slow but we made it. It took Harry a bit longer to pack his bike than it took to pack my hack (Whooo it rhymes!)
I was having fun on the hack as I slowly learned how to slide. But it was still scaring the hell out of me most of the time, because 90% of the slides were not intended. Like 'What the hell was that?" type of slides.
I was not even close to know what I was doing, but I was giving it my best. Later that morning, I was sliding sideways in corners and having a ball.......10% of the time! By the time the road was climbing around Christina Lake it got messier, but at least the views were unbelievable! Last year I was in awe at the beauty of the winter scenery from a helmet's perspective, and I was feeling the same way this year! This is so cool!

Christina Lake BC

Things started to deteriorate quickly after this

The snow was getting thicker by the "Holy crap" minute

So far I was only wearing my Aerostich Darien pants with my polar tech Long john's and my Darien Jacket with my polar tech undershirt, a T-Shirt and the Aerostich liner, and I felt warm and toasty. I had my Sorel boots on and damn! If I could have kissed them I would have!

Well! I did eventually! I don't like salt, it makes me retain water! Before we knew it, the tarmac was gone most of the time, and the wind was picking up.! As the snow gradually appeared and covered the road, we slowed down quite a bit. Harry was struggling to stay up and I was struggling with how the rig was handling.

The F%$#@ thing wouldn't turn; and when it did I felt like I was not in control. The icier it was- the harder it was to turn. The front end wanted to do its own thing and my rear end another. (My ass) And I did not like this one bit. We stopped many times to take a break and check on each other.

By then it was snowing pretty hard and we saw less and less traffic. Oncoming cars looked at us like we had four heads and perhaps we do.
While we were stopped on a hill, an RCMP cruiser stopped by. Not that we were speeding; but he just had to make sure we were not some nut cases (Well! We were!), who had broke loose from a nut house not too far. The constable could not believe his eyes! He said that in the nine years he had been around these parts

Higher! More snow! More snow! More pucker moments! More pucker moments! Less speed!

he had never seen anything like this! "HMMM I wonder why!" By that time, Harry was struggling quite a bit more and I was not sure anymore how long he was going to last. But he was hanging on! Hats off to him!

The guy had determination. While we were going up he lost it, and fell down at about 30 km/h. He was ok and the only damage his bike had suffered was on his left Touratech aluminum pannier. Nothing a bit of welding wouldn't fix! As he got back up he said "Well! Battle

Whoops!

scars!"
Man! This guy has an untouchable spirit. Twenty minutes later, the shit had really hit the fan. My hack could barely move forward, Harry was down to 10 km/h and we could hardly see where

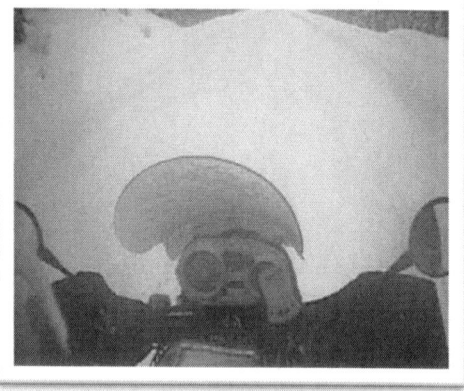

we were going! With his four-way flashers on Harry kept going but we stopped often and each time I asked him if he could still go ahead he said yes with a grin on his face. I would go for a while and then wait for him. He wanted me to stay ahead of him. He said that having me behind him made him nervous. Something to do with me filming! At one point, after waiting for him for about forty minutes I turned around and went back. I met with him about ten minutes down the road. Slow as molasses, his eyes pocking out of his skull, his shield open because he was breathing hard and it made his Schuberth fog up. Talking about fogging up, this B2SV Bombardier hel-met is a damn fine piece of hardware!

This is by far the best helmet I have ever worn!! The highest part was about to be over with, and we were moving forward. At least to Castlegar! Looking at how bad the road was getting, I already knew that Harry had to stop. I thought that he would be bummed out; but this is insane! I made

Waiting for Harry before Castlegar

it to the Chevron in Castlegar, hoping to see him soon coming down the hill on the high-way into town. Also hoping he would remember the lesson he had learned. *"Ignore the front brake! From here to Labrador there is no front brake on the bike ok?"* While I was waiting, I jacked the bike up, got my drill out and my studs, and put studs on my rear TKC 80. Shit! This tire was melting away! I guess riding the hack was harder on the rubber than I thought. It took me about an hour to put them on. While I was putting the studs on I was wondering if I should go up the pass and find him.

Putting my studs on in Castlegar

But I remembered the look he had when he told me he was nervous with me being near him, and I decided to wait about an hour. The conditions were getting worse in a hell of a hurry; and the locals who were gathering around me while I was waiting for Harry, were saying there was a heavy snow warning for the region.

Harry had made it to Castlegar

Harry showed up safe and sound about half an hour later. I was relieved to see him. He went straight to the gas pump and fuelled up Icicle. Then he walked his bike to where I was. I could see that he was done for. A mix of fatigue, broken nerves and stress! But he was still grinning. I went to him and told him point blank. *"Harry? I think this should be the end of the road for you- at least for today!" This is ridiculous and you cannot make it another mile!"* He agreed without hesitation.

As we were talking a fellow stopped by, and after the usual *"Do they know you escaped and that you are out!"* joke, he told us that there was another twenty centimetres of snow on its way. We decide to go to the Tim Horton's down the road and make a decision over a

good cup of freaking-well-deserved coffee! People were chatting with us like we were locals. I guess they are

either used to see wild winter stuff around these parts; or they are not afraid of aliens from planet Krypton! Looking at Harry wobbling his way in the parking lot on a bike that would be loaded too top heavy in summer it was obvious it was the latter!! After a soups and coffee we agreed. This was it for us! At least for today! We went to my usual little motel in Castlegar.
The Flamingo motel! Frank and Deborah know me there! Let's just say that they keep my bucket and my cleaning

Flamingo motel in Castlegar. When you stop by, just ask Deb or frank to use my washing stuff!

rages for my bike. I stop that often! And they know I am that anal! So we signed in and went in for a bit. After talking about how bad the pass could be, and how much worse it could get by the end of the day, we both agreed that I should go look at it. Hey! It is not about logic, remember! So now the plan was that Harry would stay here and wait out the storm, and I would try to go across the Salmo-Creston Pass and see what it was like up and across it and how bad things were on the other side toward Creston. Assuming I made it!

Leaving for the Salmo Creston Pass

The answer came very quickly in the form of a major 'Holy Shit" moment when Frosty slid on the snow bank in the exit ramp onto the highway.
Holy Crap! Just when I thought what we went through was bad! Another reason why I wanted to try it was because they do avalanche control at ten in the morning all over the pass, and it is not passable till noon. So Harry and I agreed that if I made it across I would phone him and let him know about the conditions. If I could not I would come back down and we would decided then. But if I made it, he would try the following day.
I was sad to leave him behind, but it made no sense for him anymore to even try. I could not help but think that the same thing could have happened to me last year. Mother Nature always wins in a situation involving two wheels and snow.
He also said that he would dump his big bag, put it on the bus and go with the minimum. I had tools, shovels, heaters and all the emergency equipment, and we could both use it, as long as we stayed together.
If he chose to continue to Labrador with me, I would carry his sleeping bag and everything else I could, to

make his bike easier to handle. At first we thought that he should carry his own things for safety reasons, but that changed.

He had already almost made up his mind about stopping in Brandon, but he would confirm with me next time we'd talk on the phone.

I was climbing the Salmo Creston pass at about 30 km/h! I was sliding and spinning all over the place! Good thing I had put the studs on! It was taking forever to climb. One thing was for sure! It was nasty because I had the road to myself! It took about thirty minutes before I saw the first rig come down!

He buried me in snow as he went by! I couldn't see crap! Well-that was another butt puckering moment! Not only because I could not see; but also but also because I was already going sideways as I rode up the pass. All in all it took me almost six hours to make 200 kilometres! Frosty was covered so much with crap and snow I was not even sure it was her anymore! But she was holding on!

After what seemed like an eternity I started making my way down! For those of you who have never done the Salmo Creston pass, it is a long way down! I picked up speed quickly, and before I knew it I was riding like if I was on a snowmobile! Off the seat sliding sideways! I was having a grand ole time! Funny how it is! I was so nervous my guts hurt, and at the same time I was having fun.

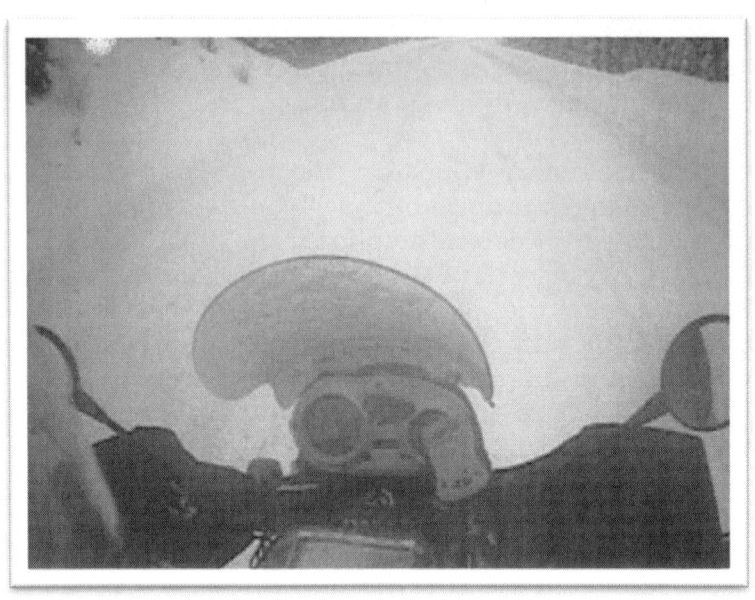

Top of Salmo Creston pass

It was wild!

It was exhausting and exhilarating at the same time. No! I will not say what I was smoking! And NO-you can't have any!

I was thinking *"Hmm! This is going to be long way to Labrador and back!* Ahhh! Paul! Shut up! No time and no point to think about that!"

I should have stopped for coffee, but all I wanted to do was keep going and clear this mess. I knew that if I stopped I would have probably just planted my ass on a chair and stayed there till spring; or until they arrested me for vagrancy! So I kept going! It was another ninety clicks to Cranbrook, and it still felt pretty damn far!

The road was still getting buried in snow as I went down the pass, and it did not stop till about half an hour past the bottom of the pass.

I just kept the hammer down (Light hammer) at about 50-60 km/h. It was all I could. The packed snow at this altitude (Lower) had turned into sheer ice, and the front wheel was dancing a bit too much when I hit this stuff! (The hack pulling me again!) And no; I will not bow down to the-I told you so-from the Ural guys!"

When I got to Cranbrook my reserve light had just come on! 236 kilometres!! Not bad considering that she normally comes on at about 350 in the dry with no sidecar.

The day had gone pretty good considering the snow storm I went through and the low speed. I wondered all day how Harry was doing! I would try to give him a shout tonight. Or like we agreed, he would leave me a message on my cell phone.

I signed in at my usual EconoLodge. I was bagged! I had spent the day fighting with the hack; and I was hacky? Remember last year in Sault St-Marie? It almost felt like it. It was good to be alive!!

Good night

Day3

Harry's notes

We left grand Forks about 7:50 AM. There was about an inch of new snow. Castlegar is about 100 kilometres away. First there was the Bonanza pass (1535 M). We hit snow and ice packed snow and more snow falling on three wheels Paul was having trouble. Me on two was having trouble. I was doing about 40 KPH and whipped out in the middle of the road. I didn't get hurt but am feeling stiff and sore in my arms but that is it.

Paul helped me to get my bike up and we continued on. I was down to about 10 KPH in first gear. For a while I got to 35 KPH then back down to 10 to 20 when it was nothing but ice and snow.

Paul eventually went up ahead and waited for me. I was easier for me this way. Finally made it down the hill to Castlegar where I found Paul at a gas station installing his studs on his back tire. It took me over 3 hours to make 100 kms. It was still snowing and there was already about 6 inches of snow.

We went to Tim's for lunch. With all my survival gear my load was quit high and top heavy. Too unstable to make it to Labrador. Paul with the sidecar his load was lower and with three wheels he couldn't fall over. Didn't make it easier to ride judging by how all over the place he was.

So my plan had changed. I will wait out this storm for a day or two and if conditions improve I will make it over the Salmo Creston pass. It's a high one.

So we went and booked in at the Flamingo hotel. Te owners are friend with Paul. Paul decided to see if he could make it up the pass before they cleared it. He headed out at around 1:00 PM. Nuts! I unloaded my bike. My left Touratech pannier was damaged when I went down. Took it in my room and hammered out the big dents and sealed it with duct tape. Paul Called about 5:00 PM. He made it to Cranbrook. He said the pass was very bad and there was no way I could have made it. He barely did. On the other side it was good compared to the pass.

He said there was a lot of ploughs working and if the snow stopped I should make it through tomorrow.

He said he would be starting late tomorrow and to call him before I leave. He'll call me tomorrow evening and tell me where he is staying. If I make it over the pass he will wait for me and we will ride to Manitoba together.

It stopped snowing in Castlegar at about 9:00 PM. I went for a walk to the highway about 11:00PM and it was softening up. The ploughs were out and it was really messy.

I repacked my bike leaving off my survival kit and anything I did not need to make it to Manitoba. I arranged to leave the stuff at the motel to be picked up later. My bike should handle better and be easier to balance without my duffle bag and the survival gear making it top heavy and light on the front. It should help me make it through.

January 4, 2008
Cranbrook BC at 23346 km on the clock

Got up this morning at seven, and took off in the dark at 7:45. The morning was nippy, but the road was clear and it had stopped snowing. The ride from Cranbrook to Sparwood was cold, icy and slippery. When I rode by the largest dump truck in the world monument, I looked at it and was thinking it would be nice to hitch a ride. But I could not find the key!
The road condition changed pretty damn quickly if you ask me. I know you didn't ask!! About half an hour (At my speed) after Sparwood, the road got covered with fresh packed and hardened chunks of slush! Perfect! It felt like I was riding in a blender! Damn that was rough!
My chin(s) were rattling, my balls felt like the lottery balls in the Lotto machine.
I kept my speed around 70 km/h. At times cars got impatient with me, but I did not give a shit! Ils peuvent bain (Bien) manger d'la marde Tabarnac! I could translate, but I won't! Needless to say that my pastor wouldn't have been proud of me; and that the Hell's Angels would have given me a membership just hearing me.
I can tell you this though! Every time I travel to Alberta I am reminded that most Alberta drivers are a bunch of fast driving, tailgating, and impatient morons that can only drive in a straight line. No nasty emails please! I kept my line and let them steam! The only ones I moved over for were the truckers. At least these guys know what the big round thing in front of them protruding out of the dash is a steering wheel.
From there to Fernie the road was snow covered mostly and not much traffic. From Fernie to Coleman it was still snow covered; but by the time I reached the Crowsnest Pass the road was dry and clean, and I stopped at the entrance of the Pass to take shots of the frozen lake.

It was absolutely beautiful. Too bad I could not find a way to go play on the ice with Frosty

It was pretty windy; but the sky was clear! Did I mention the wind was a tailwind? Yes-sir-E-Bob! Nothing to complain about! While I was stopped at the lake trying to figure out how to get on the ice and go play with the hack; a snow plough driver that had tooted his horns at me earlier, stopped and we chatted for a while.
He could not believe his eyes. He was a motorcyclist himself and thought this was freaking awesome. He told me about his rides and the roads around. I asked him to sit on my bike. He sat on Frosty and said he loved it, but; that he was happy I was the one doing this and not him. He told me I should stop at the Cinnamon Bear in Coleman, because they had the best coffee and bun in the universe!
I just could not refuse such a good suggestion. Foood! About fifteen minutes later, I was sitting in front of the most-Damn I think my taste buds are having an orgasm-Cinnamon bun. After eating it in about 2.35789 nano-seconds and drinking a good cup of coffee I had to agree with him.
The coffee was incredible. The last time I had drunk coffee this good was in the mountain of Santo Thomas in Guatemala in 2000. Man! That stuff was grown right

The Cinnamon Bear

outside the house of the Quetche people we were staying at. The mountaintops whipped by the wind were absolutely breath-taking. We do live in the most beautiful country in the world. I said it before and I will always say it. "Anyone who rides a bike owes it to himself or herself to go for a winter ride like this and see this from behind the visor " Like I said before! *No-I-will-not-give-you-some-of-the-shit-I-smoke!*

The scenery takes on a whole new personality, and it must be experienced to be believed. The combination of cold fresh air filling your lungs, the cold snapping at

your fingers while you are taking pictures, combined with the realization that you are alone out there, is something that I just cannot get enough of. You know that feeling you get on a ride, when everything is right?

The road is perfect, the curves are intimately inviting you and your machine to perform this sensuous dance that only leaning left and right repeatedly, in an almost sensual way, can create. Hold on! USSSHHHHH-Damn I rolled it tight!!

~~The scenery is exploding in front of your eyes and you almost gasp for air as picture perfect shot after picture perfect scenery goes by. You tell yourself 'Man! If I keep stopping like this I will take all day to do those 200 miles." And then you say! "What the hell!" and you just take it in. Well! In winter; take all this and multiply by a hundred.~~

Ok! Enough of that!

I cleared the foothills and stopped to take a last picture of the mountains. They are always impressive to me. They just stand there silently like a guard at the entrance of the Rockies.
These Rockies were also my biggest challenge and yet the most beautiful thing. By now a lot of the snow covered mountains are replaced by the cold, barren frozen prairies.
The snow had mostly gone but the wind and cold were making their presence known. They brought with them a stronger tailwind. This created an amazing ride. The type of ride that has you whistling tunes in your helmet and gets you a 100 MPG.
Yep! Winter riding can have its rewards. The prairies were lying ahead of me and I was looking forward to see them again. My goal was to reach Medicine Hat that night. This would be a long day in summer. But in winter it is another story! I know this and yet at that very moment on my way to Medicine Hat I caught myself relaxing in the night. Wake up Paul! Wake the hell up! Is all I could say to myself! I was more afraid this year of sliding out of control, and I had a third wheel.

The foothills

The end of the mountains and the beginning of the prairies

A third wheel that kept me upright, but also kept me day after day from being able to steer my bike the way I am used to.
I slowed down to about 75 km/h and cruised slowly into Medicine Hat. I was happy I had made it. It was late. Too late! But I was there in one piece.
I signed in, unpacked and wrote a few notes in my log, and before I knew it, I was in bed counting sheep.

One-Two-Three-ZZZZZZ!

Good night

The following is from my notes that night!

> There is something about riding in this cold. Being warm in your little cocoon brings a sense of peace and unsafe comfort. You easily forget that ice and snow are all around you. You might know when the snow is there but ice, is another story.
>
> It stalks you; it surrounds you without you noticing it. It is there waiting in the cold harsh night. Its hunting grounds take form in the shape of a curve, an unassuming hill or a crest ahead. She can count on the absolute certainty that you will be mesmerized by the beauty of her domain; and therefore unprepared! She is there; waiting with her cold silent face. Just like a predator waiting on its prey knowing too well that you are unaware of the death trap she has laid ahead of you. Her teeth cut like a razor. Her soft, silent and yet deadly moves have claimed victory a thousand times, and yet we do not learn. We simply forget she is master of her domain. And then Whoosh! You are down. What was a second ago a beautiful panorama exploding in front of your eyes or just a tunnelled view under the glare of your headlight is now nothing but a violent dance where gravity is maestro.
>
> The cacophony of crunching and cracking parts is all you can hear amidst the frightening sounds coming out of your mouth and mind.

Sometimes I wonder if my ancestors did not party-mix-whatever-sleep-attended swinger parties-with a bunch of people like Genghis Khan, Shakespeare and Freud! Oh- and Stephen King's ancestors as well!

> ***What follows is Harry's day as he goes through it. I will find this out only once I am in Moosamin Saskatchewan, two days from now!***

While I was on my way to Medicine Hat Alberta, Harry was ploughing his way through the Salmo Creston pass. He said that it took him 7 hours to do around 100 kilometres. The roads were pretty messed up. He had left his big duffle bag (Read really Huge F%$#@ bag) behind in Castlegar to be shipped to Brandon by bus. It was just too much weight sitting high on his bike and was reducing an already shitty riding condition to totally miserable.

Harry's look says it all! No words needed here!

These are the shots he took while he was making his way east to catch up with me. He said that all he could do was to stay on the shoulder where he had more traction; and even though the traffic going by him was good (As in well-behaved), he preferred staying the hell out of their way! He had the studs on, but he said he had never ridden with them till 2 weeks ago and didn't trust them yet. I told him that I could see the rooster tail of snow and ice coming off his rear tire and that he was really chewing on the snow and ice, but he still could not wrap his head around it yet. But he said that by the time he was done with the pass, that he was doing better and learning to lean a bit more.

It was open and kind of clear coming out of Castlegar, but it really got messy once he started to climb

He also had trouble keeping his visor clean. He had to stop many times to wipe the snow and fog off the inside of his helmet. Later on when I talked to him on the phone I told him to blow his air down and away from his face and to make a shield to deflect the air away. It worked! It would have made his ride a bit less ugly if he had seen where he was going.

Slowly but surely he was making his way up!

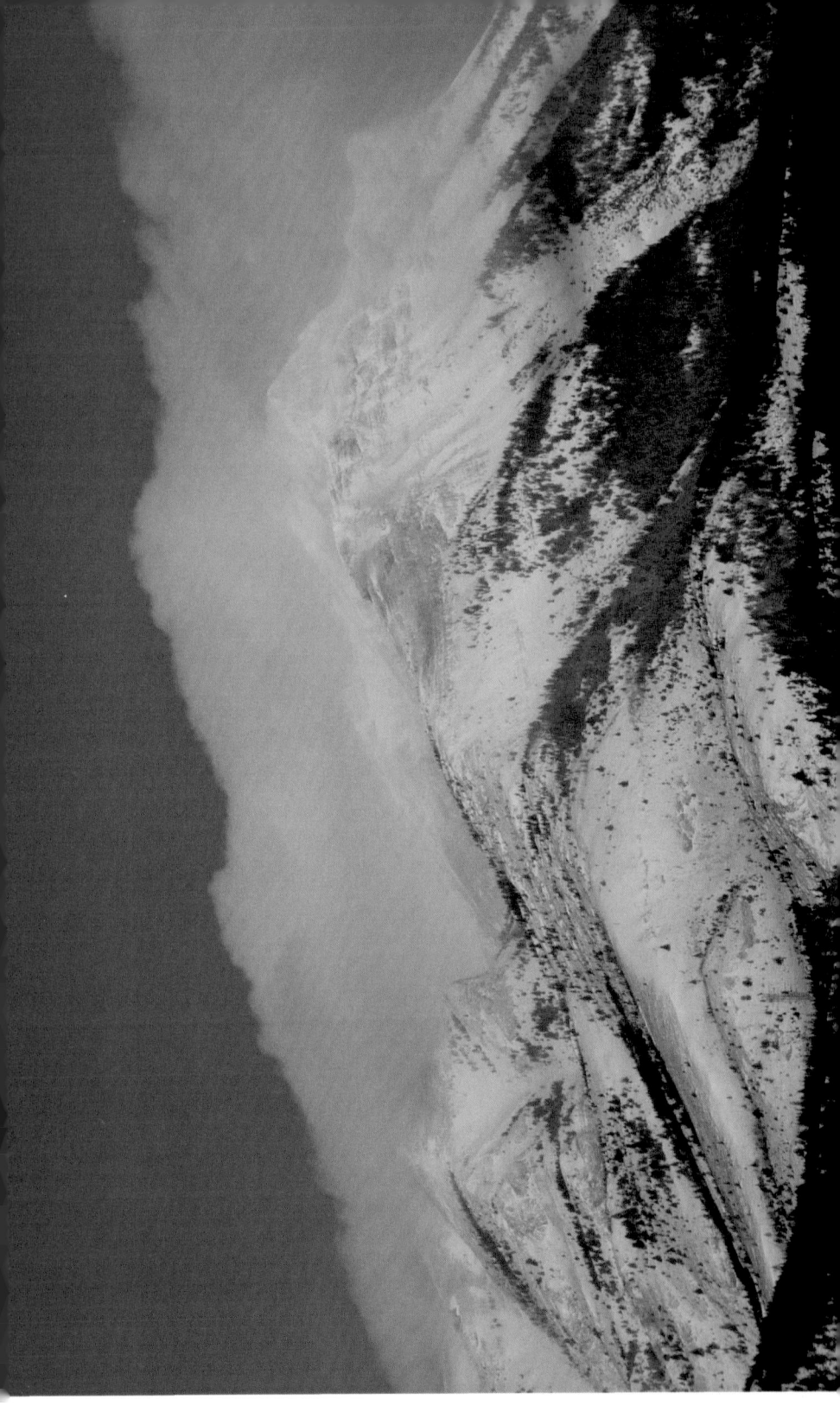

Previous pages: Foothills outside and Crowsnest Pass

From British Columbia to Alberta on Hwy 3

Harry's notes

January 4, 2008

Creston, 125 kilometres to go. I was up at 7:00 Am and walked to Tim's for breakfast. After, I walked to the highway and it didn't look too bad. I headed out at about 11:30 AM. The hill and the pass out of Castlegar were a challenge. Lots of snow and ice. It was slow going. I stopped at a gas station outside Salmo and the guy said he had no idea of the conditions of the Salmo Creston pass. I continued on and got to the intersection of Hwy 3 and 6 about 1:30 PM. I stopped and took a couple of pictures.

So I headed down the road and soon hit the pass. It is 1744 metres, the hiughest commercially used pass in Canada. The weather turned from rain to snow, to heavier snow with wind. The road changed from slush and ice to to patched snow and ice. It is a great long way to the top. Very very winter up there.

I stopped at the top for a couple of pictures, chatted with an RCMP officer up there. He didn't ask for my drvier's license. Just said to be careful anbd drove away.

Heard a dog bark. He must be a dog handler. Probably with avalanche search and rescue. I worked my way downn the pass. It went on for miles and miles with ice and packed snow. I never got ut of first gear.

Most of the way I was dragging my feet to hold myself up. I was doing 10-15 KPH. Stoppped for a rest and snack a couple of times. I took more pictures. About 16 kilometres outside of Creston the ice started to thin out and then changed to pavement and rain. I finally got out of first gear. I got to Creston at about 4:00 PM I got a motel and unloaxed my bike. I checked my cellphone anbd had three messages from Paul. He made it to Medecine hat Alberta. Holly Shit!

I called him and told him wherei was. He said the road from Creston was pretty good. Just some slush and bit of icy spots by Fernie. It took me 5 ½ hours to do 125 kms. I was done for the day.

Day 4

Medicine Hat AB, January 5th 2008
23825 KM on the clock

What the h.....? 5:57 AM? Why am I awake at this time? Was too tired to sleep last night, and now I am awake before the rooster. I'll shake my head! Maybe this is just a dream and I really just went to bed! Nope! It didn't!
I got up and looked outside-stared at the bed-looked outside-HMMMM! Nice dark sky! Stars and absolute nothingness! For Pete's sake Paul! Go back to bed! ZZZZZZZZZZZZZZZZ Done! 7:30 AM! Holy crap! Felt like five minutes! I do not want to get up! 8:00 I got out and started Frosty. She was purring like a cat. The temperature was about -20°C, and the sky east of me was just starting to be lit up by the sun.
The weather forecast was calling for colder temperatures, but at least no snowfall. After packing and suiting up, I took off towards where my front wheel was pointing. The wall!

Just kidding! As the darkness receded and the sunlight came, the wide-open prairies came to view. I am always amazed at how big they are! I have done it so many times, and still, every time the beauty and the calm soothe me. You ride, ride, and ride forever and it does not seem to want to end. Little towns line the TCH, and each and every one of them has a story. The locals also have stories to tell to whoever wants to hear them. Stories about that record breaking drought that drove some of them out of business or the one when there was just too much moisture and not enough heat.

Little towns like Piapot, Webb, and Chaplin were going by me. I stopped at one of my favourite places. Gull Lake is a one of these little towns that real travellers know; and where a trucker's breakfast was calling me!
But after experiencing this gargantuan mix of artery clogging-heart stopping-liver killing-kidney overloading-bladder inflating-taste bud caressing-but so damn good work of art many times in the past, I decided to go just

for a coffee. If I had succumbed to its call, I am sure I would still be burping by the time I reached Goose Bay!
So on through SK I went! I was not sure where I would make it that day, but Winnipeg was what I had in mind. Anything past Regina would be good. I left a message to Harry that morning telling where I was at, but I got his answering service.

Knowing him, he was soldiering on! I was hoping we'd meet at the next place I would stop at, but I would have to wait to see how it went with him first. The prairies were clear! There were many icy spots; but it was clear. It was hard to complaint. Winter-motorcycle-ice-sub zero temperatures-darkness, all these words working together and I was still here to talk about it. Yep! Nothing to whine about!
I knew I should enjoy the green vast prairies because this would most likely turn to a lot worse, once I reached the great Lakes and Ontario!
I was around Regina when the sun went down and the temperatures dropped a few degrees per minute. Ok! That is what it felt like! Focus here-Focus! It went from around -5°C to -14°C when I stopped. I kept cruising till I couldn't anymore, and it was Moosamin Saskatchewan. When this ass of mine hit the hay, it had travelled a bit over 700 kilometres that day. Not bad!

I signed in at the Moosamin Motel of course, and hunkered in! No internet though! It is one of these little Mom and Pop places I love so much. I had a message on my cell! It was Harry! He had stopped in Swift Current for the night, about 500 kilometres from Moosamin. He was getting closer.
I gave him a call. It was good to hear his voice. He was in good spirits, and despite a hellish day; he was doing great! He told me he had a horrible time going through the Salmo Creston Pass, and that he would tell me about it later.
Judging by how hard the snow was coming down when I went through the pass, I am sure it was more than hellish.

Notes from that night

I talked to Harry today and he seemed ok! But Dammit I am not! I feel bad about having left him behind. I know he can take care of himself as much as I can of me. But Tabarnac! Why am I feeling so F%$#@ guilty? Last time I felt this guilty and responsible was in 06 when Ian died.

I am looking forward to see him get here. I rode thousands of miles with people in my mirrors. The one who saw me the most in his was Ian. I would give anything to be able to see him in mine still.
Maybe this is why I feel this way about Harry! Paul! Cut the crap Sacrament! It is why!
The last time you took off with Ian, he died in front of you and you rode back alone from California. Hardest fucking ride I have ever been on. I guess I am scared to relive this as I ride with Harry! That would also explain why I felt the way I did ever since he asked me to tag along.

What if something happened to him while he was trying to catch up to me? How the hell would I feel? I am tempted to say that it would stop me in my tracks; but I can't! I have always bounced back from catastrophe before and I feel that if I were to be hit again by something like this I would....

Fuck this! I can't write or think anymore.
Good night

The following day I changed motel like I told Harry I would do. There was a bigger but more expensive one on the other side of the street, and it had internet and a nice restaurant in it.

I spent part of the day updating my blog and making phone calls. Harry was making good time, and I knew he would get to Moosomin sometimes during the day; but did not know it would be that early.

Harry pulling in at the motel in Moosomin Damn I was happy to see him!

I was sitting at the desk writing when he showed up in the window. He had first gone to the wrong motel. When he drove in the Motel's parking lot, the owner came out and said. "You must be looking for your friend! He is across the street waiting for you!"

I was pretty happy to see him safe and sound! He told me about his hellish ride going across the Salmo Creston Pass.

We ended up spending the afternoon sitting in the room drinking beer (For Harry) and I coffee. After talking about our rides from Castlegar to Moosomin, it was obvious we had two different rides. As far as Harry's ride was concerned, it was the hardest one he had ever been on. He was happy he had done it though!

We had dinner at the restaurant and tons of coffee and just relaxed. Harry sitting on his bed with is glasses on the tip of his nose writing in his journal, and I writing my journal on my laptop. What a contrast?

We hit the hay early because we know it would be a cold one tomorrow. Frosty and Icycle were tucked in away from view, right besides out room window and we were ready to roll.

I hope I won't snore the paint off the wall like I did in Grand Forks!

Good night

Harry's notes

January 5, 2008

Swift Current Saskatchewan. 801 kms

I left Creston at 6:30 AM. The road was good for a mile or two out of town then turned to slush and snow on top of a sheet of ice. It was slow again. It took me 3 ½ hours to get to Cranbrook. About 100 kms.

At one point I pulled over and stopped to let a line of traffic pass and a car stopped and a young lady asked if I was ok. That was nice of her. All the way to Cranbrook was pure ice. On the way out it was just wet pavement.

There was one patch of ice between Cranbrook and Fernie. It was about 2 miles long and nasty. I made it through. It took about an hour to make it from Cranbrook to Fernie. After a stop for gas and a Tim's I headed out.

The road was wet with some slush and ice in shady places. I went east of Coleman in the Crowsnest pass. I pulled over because I saw something on the road and I didn't know what it was. Turns out it was dry pavement, a bit white from the road salt.

After I got out of the Crowsnest pass the highway was dry. Look at that what is that? Second gear. I continued on to Swift Current and got there at about 9:30 PM.

I called Paul and he was at Moosomin Sask. He said he would stay there and wait for me. I had a good ride today except for the icy parts. I was warm but my arms and butt were sore. It is supposed to be a bit colder tomorrow so I put the liner in my jacket and pants on.

Day 5, 6

Moosomin SK, January 6th and 7th
Mileage 24509
Left Moosomin SK and rode to Dryden Ontario
Arrived at Ron's at 6:30 PM

We got up bright and early and rode while it was still pitch black out there! We could see the stars in the sky like they were right there just a few feet away. As we rode, we slowly saw the sun come up in front of us and light up the sky. Shades of purple, pink, orange and blue made the sky look like it was on fire.
Seen this many times in summer but the cold winter air as we know makes the sky so much clearer.
We were riding side by side for a while and we would often hunk at each other and give the thumbs up as we pointed at the changing sky.
The sun shining on the frozen road, the trains going by on the endless tracks, spewing a thick white cloud of steam, and the grass shining with ice made for picture perfect scenery! It was a glorious ride.
Two friends sharing a perfect adventure! I wouldn't have traded it for anything. The only part I did not like was leaving Harry in Brandon Manitoba!
I enjoyed my time with Harry! He is a hell of a guy! I do believe nothing can bring him down.

We spent about an hour at the Tim's joking around with some of the locals who simply sat down with us at our table. While Harry and I were at the Tim Horton's I noticed that my mud flap was hanging funny. I walked outside and found that a part of it broke off somewhere between Saskatchewan and here. A bolt had fallen off! And while one side was hanging down, and the other was still bolted on, it rubbed on the tire and pretty much ground the plastic right down to nothing.
I guess the sideways forces caused by the sidecar were too hard on the frozen plastic. So off it came-and in the garbage. We eventually made it outside, gave each other a big hug and we parted.

Harry in Brandon Manitoba

***It had been an honour to do this trip
with him***

Harry had made it home safely, and I felt privileged to have done something like this with him. From there I kept a steady pace toward Dryden. I stopped for gas at Falcon Lake, which is a snowmobile Relais in winter time. Frosty blended right in!

I also stopped at Kenora's Husky truck stop where a cup of coffee was in order! It was cold but dry and not much traffic. While I was riding a few people phoned me and invited me to their place in Winnipeg! I chose not to stop because I was making good time and wanted to be in Dryden early in the trip.
The memory of last year's event around the Great Lakes is still roaming through my mind and I do not want to go through this again. As tough and scary as it was I am sure it would be worse with the sidecar.
Sorry! Thanks to the guys at Wildwood Motorsports in Winnipeg and my friend Ina's sister as well. Thank you so much for your hospitality offer. I will try to make up for it when I come back.

Harry and I in Brandon! Two friends, two bikes, one country and one winter.

It does not get any better than this.

It was about 7:00 pm when I reached Dryden. Ron and his wife had dinner ready for me and as usual it was a king's meal. I know I will probably get some hate mail from the vegetarians! Hey! Can't please everyone!

I like to eat things that had a face and a mother. I like my meats and Ron does too. So it was not a surprise then I got there and Ron told me he had his usual meal ready. A slab of cow the size of Ontario! I am not saying to anyone reading this book should stop at Ron's in Dryden, but if you are in his parts of the woods and get to meet him, you will not only meet a hell of a great guy but also in my opinion THE ambassador of the northern Ontario motorcyclists family. Ron! What can I say? You are a scholar and a gentleman!

slab of cow and all the trimmings at Ron's place.

Ron has been parts of these winter trips from the moment they were being planned. Plus- I have always stopped at Ron's on my way across Canada since the day I met him on the road around Dryden in 2004. It is my second home. I wanted to leave the following morning and take advantage of the fact I was slightly ahead of a weather system that kept hanging on my ass.

Snow started falling early at night and kept going all night. Frosty was outside for the night and as usual I hated that. But her freaking appendage kept me from bringing her in Ron's garage. I spent part of the evening with Ron and Tanya and hit the hay early. I had a long day ahead of me and needed the rest. The last picture I saw that night was the forecast on Ron's big screen TV showing what was coming. Somehow I slept pretty good!

This year I had decided not to let the Weather Channel's forecast bother me................ too much!

Good night

Frosty parked for the night in Dryden

Harry's notes

January 6, 2008

I was up at 6:30 and on the road by 7:07. The roads were good I cruised at 90 KPH or so. The sun came up at 9:01. I had breakfast at Tim's in Moose jaw. I put on my electric vest to try it out. It was warm and toasty.

More heat than I needed, so I just turned it on and off every half hour or so. My face was cold because had to have the visor open a crack so it wouldn't fog up. I arrived at Moosamin at 1:00 PM and found the motel Paul was at. It was great to see him again. He out my pictures on the internet and we went for lunch to catch up on our stories.

Harry's notes

January 7, 2008

We were up before 6:30 and on the road shortly after 7.it is only about 150 kms to Brandon. It was -17°C this morning we were nearly in Virden Manitoba before I turned on my Electric vest. It warmed me up so nicely. Bring on -30°C.

We stopped at Tim's in Brandon for some breakfast. Someone took a picture of Paul and me in front of the Tim's before we parted ways.

Note: the ride was a great experience, especially doing it with Paul. I think I would do another one if I a good reason to. The next time I would have a better helmet and way more studs.

Day 7

January 8th, 2008
Left Dryden at 10, 11 AM
Rode to Nipigon and arrived 25589 kms

Waking up Frosty in the morning

Snow fell through the night in Dryden and Frosty got covered with a white blanket. When I got out in the morning getting ready to leave, I looked at her and I felt bad for leaving her outside like this.
She reminded me of a Husky sleigh dog sleeping in the snow. This is how I will look at her every morning. My faithful friend resting peacefully in the snow.

I had coffee with Ron! (While I was sleeping he went to Tim and got us some coffee! What a guy!) After shaking off the webs wrapped around my still sleeping brain cells, I gathered my crap and we went for breakfast at the Central hotel restaurant. Then I took off while Ron was making some footage of me riding. We stopped again at a little place I had stopped last year.

Above: Packing In Dryden

Below: leaving Dryden after breakfast

Above: January 2008 No Great white north sign

Below: "Great white north" sign

Ron doing what he does best

Keeping an eye on things making sure everything and everyone is ok!

Below: My first ADV Rider sticker.

> **NOTE:** Those two guys who had this show on Canadian TV twenty years ago about two Canucks in the north (Can't name them) have coined the term and prohibit anyone from using it because they have the right to it. How freaking sad is that? After seeing the picture (Bottom one) on the internet, they forced the owner of the store to remove it.
>
> To those two guys I say this on behalf of all Canadians who love and travel through it.
>
> "Fuck you!" or in my language "Mange d'la marde!" This is my/our country! Not yours! And this country is known worldwide as the 'Great white north" Caught me! I said it! Whoowhoo! 'Great White north! Na! Na! Na! Nana! Na!
>
> So unless I am mistaking, you do not own this country. Maybe in your mind you do-but you don't!

I put my Aerostich back on because even though it was around -20°C, it was still too warm for my North 49 suit. I said goodbye to Ron and took off. About an hour outside Dryden (Just like last year) snow started falling and the road got covered in a hurry!

The road conditions constantly changed as soon as I left Dryden. There was a lot of wind and I was fighting this thing like a pig in a mud pile. My arms got tired early in the day and my mind was getting tired too. I got frustrated fighting the wind continually. Somehow it felt as if Frosty was losing power by the minute. She ran fine, sounded good, and there were no signs of trouble, but she didn't feel like her usual self.
I pulled over in on a little deserted side road and after crawling in the snow around her, I discovered that

somehow the rear wheel had gone out of adjustment and the chain and sprockets were not lined up anymore. I inspected the sprocket (Rear) and it had been damaged quite a bit. Maudit Tabarnac de colisse de sin crème de sœur blindée de crisse!

I thought that this new chain and sprocket would make it to Goose bay but it looked like this little mishap (My f%$@ up) had shortened their lives Tabarnac! Well! It could have been worse! A lot worse! I got the tools out and readjusted the wheel. While I was there I jacked up the rig and lubed the chain while it was warm!

I know! I know! It was warmer than if I had done it first thing in the morning.

When I got to Ignace the road was starting to be covered with rough icy patches, and covered with snow at times. The sky turned to grey very quickly. I knew what can happen in these parts when the weather takes a turn for the worse and I was not looking forward to an Encore. I could see the snow coming slowly toward me and I knew there was no way out of this mess. I took a break, checked everything on Frosty and took off. It looked nasty on the horizon.

Above: Road coming into Ignace Ontario

Below: I took a break on the side of the road before hitting the bad weather ahead of me.

I checked the chain one more time and I suddenly remembered that when I stopped in Moose Jaw to adjust my chain I had not put Lock Tite back on the adjustments bolts. I am sure the sub zero temperatures just shrunk the metal like the cold water did to my manhood on Polar Bear swim day; and they came loose. Well! Live and learn! The scenery passing in front of my eyes was beautiful. I was as blown away with it as I was last year. The bright live colors of summer were replaced by shades of grey, white and brown. The silvery shine of the snow covering the lakes as far as the eye can see makes the water look like a field covered with shimmering metal. I stopped at the same spot I did last

Can't beat this

year near Kabaigon, and took the same picture of the bay and the island frozen in their tracks.

This time I have a thermos of coffee with me. I sat on the guardrail looking at this and thought *"Dammit! We do live in the most beautiful country in the world"* As I sipped on my hot cup of Joe, the cold wind was trying its best to reach my skin and whip me into a shivering mess.

But it could not! From the warmth of my gear I realized how blessed I was to be able to do this, and be part of this winter wonderland.

As I was riding by the frozen lakes I was remembering times when my dad and his brother Jacques were driving their VW Beetles on the frozen lake where our cabin was.
They would race side by side and when they had reached a certain speed would pull on the E- Brake and spin their way to the edge of the lake. Kids in adult bodies! The day went by relatively eventless so to speak. And I was making half decent time. The road threw me a

Or this!

few curve balls, and scared the living hell out of me; but somehow the memory of last year trip was helping me keep my cool.

At one point around Martin the road literally disappeared in the middle of a curve. Even though I wasn't going fast I was not prepared for it, and could not react in time. A fluffy powdery snow had covered it completely! Suddenly I had no reference point anymore. *Sault St-Marie pucker-time all over again!*
I shifted my weight off the seat and pegged the throttle open to slide into the curve. Or at least what I thought was the curve. It took me about one and a half nanosecond to realize that my sidecar wheel had slid all the way in the right shoulder. I gunned it, pushed the

rig with my lower body at the same time; thinking this would make it turn, but I was wrong. When Frosty's wheels hit the snow bank and stopped sliding away. I regained traction and fishtailed my way back on the road. (I think) I got back in my lane just in time to see the road reappear. Pucker factor of 9.01 on the pucker factor scale.

Just this patch! Put there just to freak me out! It is almost as if a damn politician was controlling the weather. It made so F%$#@ sense whatsoever

Break time! You'd think that after so many quality moments like this that you'd get used to it-but you don't. Every one of them is different from the other. The only thing all these moments have in common is how tense certain body parts get. Was this my gut getting in a knot? Or was it my balls squeaking on the seat? Who knows!

Or maybe this?

The scenery was soothing my achy parts though. Tree with their branches heavily laden with snow looked as if they if they were saying "Ok! I surrender!"

Even Frosty somehow looked like she was resting. After about ten minutes, I took off again. Daylight was

running out of breath and the scenery was getting darker. I had no destination tonight but I was hoping to make it to Thunder Bay at least. There are a few motels along the TCH I am familiar with and wanted to stop at one of them...
Mother Nature wanted to show me a few things again. But not before she threw an incredible sunset at me.

The rays of light reaching the ice looked like a light sword and made the ice explode with colors. Just like the rainbow does in the rain! It was a beautiful reminder of why we- motorcyclist love being part of the scenery. It was the perfect sunset, in a perfect setting, on a perfect day. I guess it is all about perception, or the size of the joint you are smoking.

The road toward TB was frozen most of the time, but sometimes wet spots would appear. (Never figured this one out), and I'd slow right. What looks like a wet spot, can sometimes be a patch of shiny ice. Don't ask me how I know? Let's just say that at one point on my trip last year there was a piece of seat covering that got sucked up my ass as I learned this lesson. About an hour or two before I got to Thunder Bay a warm current in the air turn the snow into sleet making the road feel like I was riding on butter. The oncoming traffic sometimes sent toward me a wave of slush, snow and ice that hit me like a freaking wall.
It scared the living hell out of me the first time, and the second time, as well as the third time. Oh Hell! It scares the crap out of me e-ve-ry-single-time!
My shield gets covered instantly and for a second I couldn't see crap! No-hold on! All I could see was crap! I'd quickly wipe the shield (You think sand is bad for it? Try salt, sand and ice!), and keep going. Frosty was covered with so much thick grey salty crap, she made a Thanks Giving ham look sweet.. I could hardly see her color and my windshield looks like a giant dirty Mr. Freeze!
The traffic was slowing down because I was not the only one struggling with the piss poor visibility. The rigs had

it made though. They could see everything from up there and they couldn't help but splash the passing vehicles. I tried for a while to hide behind a cube van but this half frozen wave of crap reached me every time.

As I approached Thunder Bay it started to snow heavily and the big snowflakes looked more like snow balls. By now the visibility was almost down to Zip! It was about six when I reached TB and I was looking forward to stop, but not enough to stop where I had first planned. I was still pretty energetic somehow (Or freaked out?) and wanted to make it to Nipigon or further. That was not a good idea! About ten minutes out of TB the wind picked up and the big freaking flakes which were as heavy and wet as diapers were falling with a vengeance.

At one point I had to slow down to about 50 km/h. That is all I could muster because I could not see enough. Sometimes I would move over when I could and let the traffic go by! By now it was pitch black, and traffic had thinned out a bit. It was hard to see because the snowflakes were so big and clumped that it felt like freaking pancakes were hitting my shield; or that I was driving through giant popcorn machine.

Couldn't see shit! The lights in front of me, the ones in my mirror and the ones coming were blinding me and the now FUBAR visor was harder to see through. I had absolutely no tolerances for traffic that night.

I could see something coming and throwing this huge killer wave as if it was surfing, and I was screaming profanities in my helmet.

NOTE: The following is not stuff you want the kids to read about! This was written straight from my notes that night.

About half an hour out of TB there is a truck behind me! You've heard me praise them and you know how much I love them trucks and truckers. Was one, and loved it. I know it; I understand it and I respect it. But this one was tailgating me when I could not move over. At one point he is about six feet behind me, and I have nowhere to go! I slow down to about 20-30 km/h and he would not pass me. He could but would not! Meanwhile the traffic is passing us like we are stopped.

I accelerate, gain distance, then he catches up. Then out of nowhere he puts all his lights on as he is tailgating me. I am not scared but I am getting pretty fucking pissed.

So I decide to play along and just go with it. Just keeping ahead of him enough!

45 minutes go like this, and he will not pass me. At one point I yelled in my helmet *"Ok! I have had enough of you-you Mother fucker!*

We are going up a hill, it is snowing, it is slippery and I am pissed off! I slow down so much I am sure we could have walked faster! It is one lane and we are (For now) just him and I!

I pull over hoping he will just pass, but NOOOOO! He stops right behind me on the shoulder with his hazards on! AH-AHHHHH! Play time! I stay on my bike; he gets out of his truck and walks toward me. A guy in his 50's, with a huge beer gut, and I could smell him even though it was windy!

He comes right by me and says! What the F%$#@ are you doing on the road? You don't F%$#@ belong here asshole! Get off the F%$#@ road or I will get you off the road myself!

I turn and tell him "I am doing 90 clicks at times you moron, what the hell is your problem?"

You he says! I undo my helmet, take off my baklava and get off my bike without saying a word! I can't, he won't F%$#@ stop yakking! We are both standing on the shoulder and I am just listening! I am thinking he will run out of breath and just move on! Plus I am too tired for this fat piece of shit!

Then he moves toward me, as to grab my jacket. I have my helmet in my right hand. Well! I don't know what happened but somehow my helmet made contact with his ugly face and he fell backward in the ditch!

Now the funny thing is that he is flat on his back, his feet up the little hill in the ditch with his upper body pointing south! Oh Yeah! And there must be 3 feet of snow!

Therefore Mr Fat ass could not get up. He is starting to roll and trying to get up but he is struggling-plus he is not dressed for snow games! His big belly is flopping all over the snow, his shirt is riding up his back, and he just can't get up!

At that very moment I am thinking! This would not be the right time to leave a man in the snow alone! So I stay while he is grunting, mumbling, swearing and I think..... Farting!! Yep!!! After about four or five minutes of watching Butterball do the frozen bacon dance, he finally gets on his feet! Not out of the ditch yet, but at least, he on his feet. Snow glistening off his gut like frost on Heineken keg! He is just about to come up and start yelling at me A-G-A-I-N!!!

I am standing right there in front of him, watching emerge out of the ditch like Moby Dick out of the ocean; and then he gets closer. I raise my helmet which was on the ground, I put my gloved fist against his chest and I tell him *"Man! Do not say a fucking word? Walk away and drive off! If you don't? I promise you will not get up the next time I hit you! Do you fucking understand that? You got it? Look at my bike? Look at my plate, and make damn F%$#@ sure you memorize it! Because next time, I will leave you in the fucking ditch to freeze to death! Got it?"* So! Mr Arnold Brothers transport! If you read this! I hope the crack of your butt thawed out in your Big Volvo rig!

End of the notes

There you have it! My main event of the day! Shortly after that I entered Nipigon! It would be my home for the night.

I stopped at the first motel I saw on the side of the road and pulled over. The owner who happens to be a motorcyclist as well could not his eyes! He says to me *"I thought I was tough riding in November when it is –5 and telling all my friends to stop being pussies and try it. You just shut me up!"* He gave me the special "crazy "MoFo" rate because he said I deserved it..

Thank you Sir! I walked to my room where I took a peel off and walked back outside to unpack Frosty. Damn! The cover was frozen solid. Felt more like a piece of steel! The thing was so stiff I wondered if I would need a cutting torch to take it off. All the snap broke off but three when I undid the cover.

Frosty was so filthy; it broke my heart. I wanted to wash her so bad. I knew that doing that would not be good for her.

After struggling to unpack my video stuff and bringing it inside, I grabbed a long warm shower and off to beddie bye I went. I was bagged! I couldn't have gone one more mile, even if I wanted to. Thunder Bay had taken the best out of me and I know Butterball had not helped either.

My goal was to hit Sault St-Marie the following day. Not sure though! It was snowing like crazy, and the motel owner was saying that it was supposed to pick up seriously overnight, and go on like this for a couple of days. Well! Nipigon is nice place to hang out for a couple of days if I had to.

Good night!

Day 8

January 9th, 2008, Nipigon, Ontario
Leaving at 8:00 Am

Okee Dokee! I slept TB and Butterball off! It was 7:00 AM when I woke up. I looked outside and it was still snowing and windy. We got quite a bit of it, but at least the roads seemed clear. This meant only one freaking thing. Damn cold! And damn windy! I opened the door and stuck my barely awake ass outside.
Holy shit it was cold! After a good shower and a cup of coffee (Motel coffee) I was ready to go. I walked outside, and started Frosty. By the sound of her this was the coldest morning we had hit so far.

While she was warming up I packed her. I could not help but think of how more precise and how much more a ritual my morning routine had become. I guess what I learned last year was sticking with me in many ways.
By the time I was packed up Frosty's idling still sounded pretty rough. I looked on my thermometer on my tank bag and it was now showing -30°C. You could freeze the balls off a brass monkey.
I stood in the doorway and unzipped my suit to make sure I wouldn't sweat my French Canadian ass off while she was also waking up.

The Tacka Tacka Tack Tack sound was slowly going away, which was my cue that Frosty was warming up nicely.
I walked around her and checked for things that could have come lose or broken off. The chain looked like hell. It looked like all the links were welded together. Actually it feels like it too when I take off in this cold. It takes a few minutes to warm up. THIS is the ultimate test for a chain. By the way! RK? Your chain has failed miserably. Hmmmm! Maybe I could contact DID and see what they think.

Note: This is my second trip as you know, and I have learned a trick or two about chain maintenance. There is nothing on this earth that will keep a chain from wearing out faster in extreme salty and sandy conditions, but you can help it last longer by doing a few things.

Lube: No wax type! I found out that in cold it just solidifies and flies away in no time; leaving the chain exposed and you can hear it rust as you go!

I have tried all sorts of lubes on my first trip and they have all failed. Mind you-it is was better than using none, but they did not fare well. Te only thing that has succeeded was Amsoil MP Metal Protector®

This stuff is unbelievable! It sprays on light and clear and thickens into a yellowish film that cannot be washed away unless you use a light petroleum product like Varsol or kerosene. It is bullet proof. Naturally being sandblasted like it was during this last trip made it go away. But it stayed on all day. I use it in summer and the results are simply amazing. It says it right on the can that it is good for motorcycle chains. You can also spray it in areas where it is hard to reach and where moisture goes often like all these nooks and crevasses that are so hard to reach when you clean your bike. A year and a half later it is still on and protecting Frosty.

Adjustment: Because cold temperatures shrink metal, keep your adjustment on the loose side. Your chain will not only last longer, but will also warm up faster, hence making it easier on it. Obviously not everyone will ride 9000 kilometres in snow, sand and salt, but the chain I put on in Toronto made it to Goose Bay and back to Quebec and went on for another 10,000 kilometres. Considering what it went through, I would say that using Amsoil MP and keeping on the loose side did a damn good job!!!

It was -25°C whether n I took off and it went up to about -20°C when the sun peered over this the horizon, lighting up this perfectly blue sky. Damn! I was thinking that if it kept going I would have to break out the suntan lotion and my black T-shirt with "What are you looking at?" on it. I was almost starting to hope that Mother Nature might finally cooperate with me.
Then I told myself to stop dreaming and take whatever was coming.
Somehow I am having trouble waking up this morning. I felt as if my brain was still on my pillow back at the motel. I had woken up absolutely welded to the mattress. As I rode away I thought of what Ron had told me about the crappy weather coming in from the Great Lakes and looking at them he obviously was right.

I stopped for coffee later on and started looking on the map for an alternate route to Labrador. Not many; unless I wanted to make a detour to Fort Lauderdale! I could take route 11, but I wasn't keen on that idea. This road is so lonely in winter that the moose have started an online dating site called HOMO.com (**H**orny **O**nline **M**oose **O**rganisation). *Sorry! That is all I could come up with! I'd like to see you try!"* Moving on!

After a few hours I rolled into one of my favourite places. Schreiber Ontario! I love this little place. Good food, good motel and the waitress is French Canadian. What more can you ask for?

I stopped in here last year after a scary freaking day. The owner (Birgit! Real wonderful) took a picture of me, and put it on her wall of fame (for special travellers) this time I returned the favour.
She remembered me as soon as I walked in; and so did the waitress Sylvie who had served me. Had a good breakfast and went on my way! I have stopped here every time I have crossed Canada. And it is every year! This place screams "Motorcycle friendly!" Some of the locals that were there last year also remembered me; and are just as stunned to see me ride in as they were

last year. When they found out I was on my way to Labrador it kind of got quiet in there. *"HMMM!! Isn't that way up there at the end of the road in eastern Canada near the polar bears??"* one of them asked.

In Schreiber Ontario with Birgit, the owner of the Esso restaurant/ motel

I say "Yep!" he said *"you know? Last year when I met you I really thought for a moment that you were nuts! Now I really know!"* The wind was blowing hard out there. A cold quiet but strong wind! Just like the snake crawling on the ground. You cannot hear it but you can feel its bite! Last year when I was here the condition were a bit warmer. Now it was about −18°C and the road was still a mess. I did not have to read the rigs' wheels to know that it was cold and snowy where I was heading; and that the roads were not slushy at all. The rigs' wheels looked like giant sugar covered donuts.

After a good meal I looked outside and it was snowing a bit. I quickly opened the door and stuck my still burping self outside for a minute to see how cold it was. Holy crap! Never mind the crap! *Holy Shit! Is it cold? Or is it*

f%$#@ cold! I had no thermometer because the one in my tank bag started to FUBAR more often than not, but it sure felt like below -30 with the wind.
I heard myself whine saying *"I am tired! Why don't I just call it quit?" I can park the bike here till spring and come back and pick her up when it is warm! Where is this really going to take me?"* "Ahhhhhh! Shut up Paul!" I started getting dressed and walked outside. I hit the starter button and Frosty came to life with an offbeat rhythm. I let her warm up for fifteen minutes or so. After I was done suiting up; I went out and asked Frosty to hang on and told her how well she is doing!

There was still daylight outside by the time we were ready to leave, but I could see the horizon getting darker by the minute. Reaching Sault St-Marie would be a tough one!
As the end of the day approached the wind picked up even more, bringing snow along for the ride. Nothing like being thrown like a rag doll around the great lakes at this time of the year!
I was learning the hard way (Again) that the wind is not sidecar friendly and that you have to fight with it.
I was trying to keep my mind busy by focusing on other things like, power slides. I was starting to really enjoy these slides at highway speed, but the cagers looking at me coming out of a curve at 90 km/h sideways with a huge grin on my face did not seem to like it as much as I did. I rode for a couple of hours, non-stop; and I was bagged.
Not good! I felt like pulling over at the next motel and calling it quit. I also know I was tired when I started thinking about stuff that is not healthy. The past, failed relationships, deaths, loss of loved ones, and what could possibly happen to me during this trip and how........
"God Dammit Paul! Shut the hell up and keep going?" it is not the time, nor the place to go on this psycho babble shit. While you are thinking about things that are pointless and useless you are not focusing on what counts!

Like...................Hum! Staying alive?????"
those moments spent talking to myself were occurring more and more; and they really helped.
Now- if someone could have heard me, they would have probably called the asylum and asked them to pick me up. I stopped many times along this part of the TCH. Some of the view points and rest areas are just amazing.

Little break from the wind

The views are? Well! You have to see it to believe it. *"I am repeating myself here!"*
I do not know about you, but the space in my helmet is where I do my best thinking. It is a good place to chat, figure things out. But during this trip, concentration is mainly what is going on in there. And doing otherwise would be hazardous to my life. I try to leave this other stuff that takes too much of my attention away from road for my room at the end of the day.
Not knowing what will come tomorrow and not knowing if I will be able to go any further is tiring. But not knowing what lays ahead the next curve or whether or not you will make this damn curve is really stressful.

At times things were on the iffy side

I was more used to this ongoing feeling this year, but it still got to me at times. Fear! Constant fear is a feeling that is hard to explain. At times I was thinking about quitting right there and then. But what would have been the point of that? I have learned the hard way that I alone cannot control everything in this life of mine. And when it is just too freaking much; I have learned to rely on what some would call "Higher power", but I call Him God, or "The big guy"
There has been many times so far in this trip when I needed help had my talk with the big guy up there, asking Him to look over me one more day.
Thanking Him for this one, and also asking him for one more.
Every moment of this trip was unsafe and dangerous in so many ways; I just cannot put it in words. But! Oh yeah! There is always a "But"--It might sound macho- and excuse me for not giving a crap; the adrenaline rush was—well-HUH!-a rush! Going through this country in the most hostile conditions brings you to life in ways that cannot be expressed on paper...

The intense stress and absolute concentration you need to go through the TCH in winter, one kilometre at the time; make you feel like you are on fire inside. How else can I explain the weight loss, the aching muscles, the tensed jaw and the sore legs?

As I climbed up the higher elevations the snow level increased a lot and so did the fun! The scenes were like Christmas post cards, and I just couldn't stop taking pictures.

Yep!

When I hit White River, the home of Winnie the Pooh; Poo? Pooh! (Whatever!), I stopped for a coffee at a little coffee shop and had a cup of black plasma. It was not Juan Valdez's quality; but it did what it had to do. Half an hour later I was back on the road and the wind had also had an injection of plasma because I will be damned if it had not doubled in the half hour I was inside. And did I mention it was not (NOT) a tailwind? It is either head wind or side wind. But Hey! I was still out there, and the traffic was pretty much absent. All in all; not bad! The beauty of the scenery kept me busy. The Great Lakes can be tough in summer and let me tell you this! Holy Crap! I said that already- didn't I? Well- humour me here ok? Put up with my senility? The winds live in these parts all year around. At one point I pulled over and went on a little Park road that was closed. I had to take a break from the wind. Here is how I know winds are here all year around.

I am sure the Big Goose just wanted to take off.

Finally! Wawa was approaching. To me this normally means I have about three before I get to Sault-St-Marie. But then 'normal' is nothing but a cycle on a dryer!

I stopped in Wawa and took a picture of my friend "The Big Goose". She and I were the only two birds out there. I stopped at Timmy and had a coffee and a bowl of soup. I did not want to dawdle along too much because I knew that the snow storm was not too far. Twenty minute later I was back on the road. Where was I?
Oh yeah! Pancake Bay! The spot where last year I was thrown in the oncoming traffic lane by the wind, was coming up ahead of me. I remember it like it was yesterday! "It was dark, snowing like hell, and I couldn't

see where the hell I was going. The road was gone, and I had to drag my feet to feel the road. The next thing I know, I was riding in the other lane heading for the ditch; and there was nothing I could do! Long story short; I somehow saved it.

Now a year later; I knew where it was, saw it coming, and I was prepared. I slowed down, rode through it, and what da ya know-the wind was STILL there waiting for me! (Not paranoid!). And guess what? This time, it also blew me right across the lane on the other side. It did not give a crap whether or not I had a sidecar. Was the same to it?

But this time there was something a bit different.(large bit) I could see a bit more outside this time, and I could see the large chromed radiator grill of a big ole Peterbuilt lit up in the night by my headlight as I was sliding my way towards him. I was way off the pucker factor scale by then.

I tried to steer back in my lane but I could not. I thought of hitting the snow bank but there was not enough room between him and me if he stayed where he was. In his lane! Was I scared? Shit-I was more than scared! I was so startled I did not even have time to be scared. I was sure I was a goner!

But the guy behind the wheel was looking at me coming and somehow he was prepared.

He just swerved enough out of the way for me to have enough room between him and the snow bank. I was very happy he moved his 18 wheels and 40 tons a bit, instead of my two teeny, whiny little wheels and my light 500 lbs;(that is including the one pound turd I now had in my Teflon underwear) ending up wrapped around his axles

Thank you Sir! If you are reading this; I want to say thanks. You were/are a scholar and a gentleman and you so saved my ass I can even tell how much! You more than made up for Mr Butterball yesterday. After that I slowed down a bit, to about 70 km/h all the way to Sault St Marie. I was glued to the seat (with what? I won't tell) and I was as focused as a sniper's eye on his target. I rode straight to the motel in Soo. So here goes another day down the great lakes. Cold wind, lots of snow and a close call with a Pete. I also learned to do power slides on snow at 60 mph. All in all; a damn good day!

Notes:

I hit the sack early that night because I thought I was coming down with something.
I had ordered a damn good pizza, and it went down real quick. Blame it on nerves or whatever it was; but I ended up talking to RRRRALLLPPHHHH on the big white telephone.
What a waste of money!

Good night!

Little side road adventure

My track were the only ones on it

Day 9

January 10th 2008
Arrived in Sault St Marie last night at 29290 kms on the clock at 6:45 PM local time
Leaving Sault St-Marie for Toronto at 8:00 am

It is 6:30 when I got up and the first thing I did as usual was to look outside. The weather had deteriorated, and the sky looked like it was ready to dump a big can of whoop ass on me. Last year when I was here they had closed the TCH on me because of the season's first snow storm that got here just before I did. I was forced to stay in Soo for two days.
I was hoping that I wouldn't go through this again. Looked like now I would be able to leave and make some miles. How much- I did not know because the crap that had been coming from the US was still very faithfully riding my ass. I was told that Toronto was going through the mildest winter in history.
No snow there- whatsoever. Maybe I would be able to suntan while BMW Toronto worked on Frosty and gave her some sugar...
I stopped in Bruce Mines for breakfast at the Bobber's restaurant for porridge and hot coffee! It does not get any better than this. This picture was taken by Captain 90 on my 2007 trip. Same place! Same season!

At Bobber's Restaurant in Bruce Mines Ontario

Same nut! It is a very nice place even in winter. I stopped last year to meet Captain90 from the CanadianXRiders.ca. It is the type of place motorcyclists like to stop at. Right on the side of the road with a patio looking at Lake Ontario's North Channel. Great food, great parking, and great prices! And NO! They do not sponsor me. But as you already know; I like good food and motorcycle friendly places. I know hundreds of them in Canada and the US. HMMM! Maybe I am onto something here." **The motorcyclist guide to good eatin!"** After a good breakfast I was ready to roll.

The road was mostly clear and dry, with just a few icy patches in the shaded areas. Each time I hit one of these; it scared the crap out of me. Not because I was losing control; but because the sidecar reacts differently on ice. Normally with just her two wheels, Frosty would lose traction a bit and probably fishtail a little. On the other hand, the sidecar rig veers to the right. I suppose it is because the car's weight, which is being pushed by the bike, suddenly pushes the bike as the bike loses traction. Hey Ural guys! Jump in anytime to help me make sense of this! It felt like I was about to start making a donut at 90 km/h. Not fun! I am not used to this and most likely will never be; because I am not a sidecarist and never will be.

The wind had picked up again. I had to stop because Nature was calling. I stopped in Thessalon at the same little restaurant I always stop at for coffee. After resting my arms and shoulders for twenty minutes, I got back on the road. I was still amused by the look of the drivers as they came towards me.
I made it to Blind River and by then the wind has started to get to me again! I was still talking to myself in my helmet saying things like *"I am so fucking tired of this. Why won't you stop you piece of shit? Why don't you just give me a break!"* and all the nice French Canadian swears in between.
Nothing another cup of coffee, and a chocolate chip cookie can't fix! Hum! Make that two cookies!. There are a lot of French speaking people in that area and I chatted with a couple of guys who had put their bikes away for the winter and wondered what the hell I was doing here in January
I told them that if I had to explain; they would not understand. They looked at me funny and somehow

walked away. Good! I was too tired to go on and on about why I was doing this. To be honest, at this moment I didn't know myself.
While Frosty was outside being looked at by a few people, I got dressed and walked outside. Another ten minutes chatting with kids outside, and I was on my way. The road between Blind River and Spanish is pretty much the last bit of road going alongside the water for a while, because it goes inland from here.
I like all of the TCH but this part is not as pretty as the others. Maybe it is because you spent the last 3 days around the Great lakes and you feel spoiled a bit. Ahhhhhh! I am just whining!

The road was nice and clean and not much ice from then on, except in shaded spots, which caused some serious pucker level moments; but nothing that filled my Teflon underwear. Funny how someone gets used to do dangerous stuff day in day out; and gets to a point where, what was nuts the day before; is now just routine. I went through little towns where that go as quickly as they come. Towns like Mississagi, Spragge, Serpent River, and Spanish. The frozen lakes (Small ones), bays and rivers went by, reminding me that it is winter, even if I am comfortable with what I am doing.

When Nairn Center appeared, I pulled over and stopped at the truck stop I use to stop at years ago, to buy some gum. I needed to chew on something. Somehow my jaw was clenched and my teeth were hurting Dammit! You know you are tensed when two of the three orifices you have are hurting. Too tensed and stressed with this damned wind! Then came Whitefish, Naughton and Lively!
By the time I hit Lively I was not lively anymore. I have to admit that somehow I was not enjoying this trip at this time. Blame it on two days of fighting with the wind; and the uncertainty that built up as I saw the skies get darker and darker, and the snow falling on the horizon. I knew better than to let this get to me but I couldn't. As I got farther east I started worrying about Labrador.

I shouldn't have but I was! My mind went wild again, and I started imagining the worst. I knew that when this happens it is time for me to take a break and focus. I had started to count the miles left to Toronto and each miles felt a hell of a lot longer. I needed a rest right freaking now..

At that point safety had taken a kick in the butt and my concentration was quickly dwindling down to nothing. I was not too far from Hwy 69 turn off in Sudbury!
To me this place on the TCH has always been a turning point. It is like I can say that another chunk of Canada is behind me and that I am making progress.
As I rode by the intersection I couldn't help but think of the summer of 2004 when my buddy Sandy Goodall and I crossed Canada together.
He had to go to Toronto and I was going to Montreal. We were in Sudbury and this was where we had to part. Him going on 69 South and I, on Hwy 17 East. So we stopped at the intersection where both of them meet and we took a break. Sandy and I always did the same thing when we stopped
We'd get off our bikes; and out would come the towels and the Pledge. We would give them a quick "Debugging" as we call it; and wed chat and laugh as we proceeded with this customary habit. We would do this every time we stopped. At the end of the day it would take no more than ten minutes to thoroughly clean the bikes. Yep! We are anal! And your point????
I have always been like this and those who ride with me know it. Most of them are now infected with the Pledge disease. But that time Sandy got off this bike and ran up toward the rock cliff (Real cliff) and quickly made his way up.

As he went up I asked *"What's up?"* he said *"Got to go!,* pointing at his ass. Let's just say that when he came back down saying *'"Sorry! I had to take a dump right freaking now!"* he looked like he was 5 pounds lighter. Today there was no Pledging, and there are no bugs either. I hear -20 does something to bugs!! But the thought of Sandy climbing the rock wall at mach 2 just got me giggling in my helmet and lightened my mood up; which was really needed! So here I was at one of the dividing parts of this big country of ours.

These parts to me are like steps. I can associate how many more miles I have left and how much time I have left till the next step. And these parts, depending of the time of year I travel, are also directly tied up to weather. With these three pieces of information, I can pretty much guess close to an hour or two how long it will take me to go across Canada. I shit you not!

These parts are, from Victoria to Castlegar BC
From Castlegar BC to Medicine Hat AB
From medicine Hat to Kenora Ont
From Kenora Ont, to Sault St-Marie. This last part is over 1200 kms and represents 1/4 of the distance travelled from Victoria to Joliette PQ (My Hometown)
From Sault St-Marie to Mattawa Ont
From Mattawa Ont to Joliette PQ (easy day) this pretty much represents my 5-6 days going to Montreal.

If I go to Newfoundland via the Gaspe Peninsula I have a few more parts like this.
From Joliette PQ to Riviere Du Loup PQ
From Riviere Du Loup to Matane PQ
From Matane PQ to Mont St-Pierre
From Mont St-Pierre to Chandler
From Chandler to Campbellton
From Campbellton to Miramichi NB
From Miramichi NB to Rustico Bay PEI
From Rustico Bay PEI, to Antigonish (exit PEI via the Wood Islands ferry) to Merigomish around the peninsula, and then to Antigonish.
From Antigonish NS through Cape Breton to Cape Breton Island National Park
From Cape Breton Island National Park to North Sidney NS to catch the ferry to Port Aux Basques NL

Sleep onboard the ferry on the 1:00 AM ferry and wake up refreshed in Port Aux Basques. Then go to the Tim Horton's 2 minutes away from the Terminal.
From Port Aux Basques to the Gross Morne National Park campsite.
From the Gross Morne National Park campsite to Gander NL
Then from Gander NL, to St-John's NL and Cape Spear.

I always said that five weeks was enough to make a coast trip. Come back from St-John's NL via the Argentia ferry to North Sidney NS (Don't forget the Avalon peninsula) then go to Yarmouth NS to take the world's fastest aluminum Catamaran ferry to Bar Harbour ME and then cut your way to the east and then Midwest and then home west. TaDaaaaahhhhhh!

Where was I? Oh yes! January and winter on Frosty, at the turn off for Hwy 69 south, from Sudbury to Toronto; or called TO. I had a few pre-planned stops in and around TO. First, I wanted to go to my friend Tim's. I met Tim in 2006 when we were about to embark on the ferry to Newfoundland to Port Aux Basques.
He was on his Dakar, loaded like a mule, and we met inside (Of all places) Tim Horton's. We instantly connected. Tim is the type of guy who always is talkative in a very friendly and funny. I laughed so hard with him the back of my head was hurting.
He was on his way to Labrador via the ferry from Anchor Point to Blanc Sablons and then back to TO. He also had to travel at Mach 3.1 to make it back home on time, which he did.
Tim had kindly offered me to stay at his place, and offered to take to Toronto BMW as well. Good thing because I know crap about Toronto. He and his lovely wife Christina were expecting me for dinner; but I was running late. The winds were killing me, and as I got close to Cottage Country, the wind became just downright dangerous.
There were severe wind warnings on the radio and TV and I was heading right into this shit pit. By the time I

hit Pickerel Ontario the winds were dangerously hammering me. I actually had trouble steering Frosty. Many times, all Frosty could muster was 70 km/h and I was in a 90 and 100 km/h zone. You have to know that in the medical world the words anal, asshole, buttheads and ass heads were created after observing Ontarians driving. These people drive like-well- assholes.
Tailgating me and obviously losing the little minds they have. Of course it was always <u>the cappuccino drinking-late for or from work SUV driving-I did not get laid last night-my husband is an idiot-my wife is a bitch-I did not get a raise-holy shit how am I going to make my mortgage payment Goddammit-I have to pick up grocery-my wife found out about the little romp I had with Fifi on the printer at the office-my boyfriend had coffee with my husband-here goes half of what he owns and now I will have to work for a fucking living-the kids are driving me nuts in the back- is it legal to carry a gun and shoot them- fuck I forgot my cell-I am late for my flight and my period-I should have known this idiot was not fixed</u> driver

But being the good ole me I always am, I ignored them and just minded my 70 km/h business. By the time I hit 400 (Holy shit isn't there any speed limit on this black tarmac carpet leading to Hell going in Toronto, I was so tired and stressed, that I couldn't make it to TO anymore. Meanwhile Tim is waiting and dinner is ready I am sure.
At one point I said *"Enough of this crap!"* and pulled over to find a Tim Horton's or any place where they would give me an injection of coffee intravenously. Naturally the exit I took led me deep into the Ontario Bayou; where the only thing people living in multi-million dollars mansion know about the countryside is where the smell of cow dung stinking their cars up is coming from.

I stopped at a gas station to ask where was the nearest Tim Horton's or coffee shop; and the answer I got from this "I got a nose ring- I listen to Marylyn Manson

(Whatever the hell she/ he is)-I am not paid enough to know which planet I am living on-the only two words I know can either be grunted or horked-yes my hair is blue-and my lobotomized brain and newly immigrated ass do not give a shit about where anything is- was "Burger King? "HUUUUUUUUH! Don't know!"

I asked for Tim Horton's you douche bag- not freaking Burger King! What part of Tim Horton's didn't you understand in the foggy world you are in and call your pathetic life?
I walked outside after contemplating the idea of carving this moron another asshole. He (If he was a guy! It was hard to tell) was the proof that his dad jerked off in a flower pot and raised a blooming idiot. Anyway it looked to me that there was life toward the west end of that road. What I do not know is that this road ended in fucking Manitoba. About half an hour later, I saw this familiar sign! My smile came back, and my mind got filled with images of soup, donuts and coffee, instead of one of me strangling the crap out of this.... Give it up Paul! Give-it-up!

As soon as I parked, my stomach stopped growling, and even Frosty seemed to be relieved. I am sure that after this romp on the 400, if she could have talked she would have said, "Holy shit Mr. Escalade and Mrs Plymouth Voyager, can't you F%$#@ slow down? Can't you see I am trying? You F^%$# cappuccino hunting, 4X4 wannabes-ego boosting-your driver is compensating for something else-pieces of shit.
Anyway! I walked in and I sat down. Then I peeled Frosty's seat off my ass, and pushed my arms back in their sockets. They felt so pulled and tight, that when I bent my finger, my sphincter contracted. Then I got up and ordered a sandwich, a coffee. I got my ATM card out. *"Sorry Sir! We only take Master Card or Cash!"* I asked *"Since when is Tim not taking ATM cards?" We never did!* ARRRGHHHHH!
I mumbled *"Only in On-fucking-tario!* She looked at me and said sorry! Not her fault she only works there for 2

1/2 peanut and a kick in the ass per hour. As I turned around I heard someone saying "*We never took ATM in here!*" I looked at him with a look that said " *Don't you fucking start with me you moron! I am in no mood, nor do I have the energy to tell you that if your dad had not also jerked off in a flower pot he would not have raised the fine blooooming idiot you are!*" But I did not say a thing because coming from deep inside of me, in the deepest recesses of my hungry wind battered gut; I could feel a strange and weird sensation emerging, telling me that I was very close to entertain the thought of giving cannibalism a f%$#@ try!

Anyway! I sat quietly and calmed down a bit. Damn! People live in this environment all of their lives! A-ma-zing! Obviously driving in and around Toronto had stressed me out a bit, and I was becoming kind of an antisocial jerk. After a good cup of coffee and a sandwich paid with my Master Card; I was finally able to breathe without having my nostrils pulsating like a raging bull.

I phoned Tim and told him where I was, and that because I had to stop I would be late. He told me to just come down when I could, and that my room was ready for me and had made space in the garage for Frosty.

I finally reached Tim's place around 7:00 PM. It was good to see him and his wife. First time I'd met her. We sat down, had some coffee and chatted for a while. They welcomed me in their lovely home like family. Another fine example of the camaraderie that can develop between people who meet on the road! After a great but short evening I had to hit the hay. I was too bagged! I started counting cars on the 400 I would have liked to pick out with RPG's and fell into a deep coma.

Good night

Day 10

January 11t, Toronto Ontario
Heading east! Sometime today!!!

I woke to the smell of fresh coffee and breakfast mixed with the smell of dried up drool on my pillow. I felt spoiled! I gave Christina a hug as she left for work and thanked her. I wish I'd had spent more time getting to know her. Another time perhaps! BMW Toronto was expecting me. Frosty had some TLC scheduled. I followed Tim to BMW because I am as familiar to Toronto as a priest is with a strip joint! I know! I know! Some of you say I might be wrong on this! Let's not go there.

Toronto BMW will change Frosty's chain and sprockets, do an oil change, a service and check her up completely. A new tire will be put on the rear, and I will put studs on the tire as well. Even though the tire was still good and would have most likely carried me all the way to Labrador; I wanted to see what difference in wear and tear a good wheel alignment would make. The studs were hardly showing any wear. Even the mechanics said I should not change it. But I did not know how rough the TLH would be and did not want to take a chance. It turns out that the new tire, studs, chain and sprockets will make it to Goose Bay and back to Quebec with hardly any wear showing.

Frosty's appendage outside BMW Toronto

I had to leave Frosty's appendage outside for two reasons. First! It would not fit through the doors. Second! It was easier for them to work on the chain and rear without the sidecar.

Another reason was that I was writing a report about the new studs and wanted to submit an accurate one. By changing the tire even if it did not need to; I would be able to tell how the studs fair with and without a proper wheel adjustment. The studs had worn down by about only 10-15% after 5000 kilometres, and had saved the tire. The traction was incredible, they were quiet, and they did not affect braking or steering at all. The sidecar took care of this!

Naturally nothing ever goes 100% smoothly. BMW had all the parts except for the rear sprocket. But Tim came in and saved the day. He had one at home! So he went back home and got it so BMW could fix Frosty. To make a long story short I was supposed to get out of there

Studs on the Rear TKC 80 after 5000 kms

at about 2 PM, but got out at 7 PM. From one stock bolt to another, all the little problems that could happen happened. But the mechanics were committed and stayed till she was done. The security guard though did not want to wait and wanted to lock us up in the compound. I will not write the words I had for him. I said my goodbyes to Tim; promising we would get together again and went on my way. Thank you Tim! You are a great friend and I appreciate you very much.

Dave (Woodgrain) was expecting me at his house in Nappanee. Nice guy! No! Great guy! We met on the road in 2004 in the middle of Saskatchewan and we have stayed in contact through the years. He followed me the year before and this time I said I would stop. So I left TO and Frosty was running like a top. As I was riding towards Nappanee, Frosty felt a lot more powerful. The difference was in the wheel alignment. It turned out that the wheel alignment marks on the swing arm were not the same on both sides. So what I thought was a properly aligned wheel was in fact an out of whack wheel. Frosty was working overtime trying to pull herself with this problem.

She felt like she had gained 20 HP. It was great. I rode to Nappanee where I met Woodgrain at the Tim Horton's.

We sat down and shot shit for about an hour before yours truly started to yawn enough that I would cause a rift in the time/space continuum. Some sort of black hole! We went back to Dave's place where I sat down with him and his lovely wife, and by eleven or twelve I was in bed snoring the paint off the walls.

Another great day!

Good night

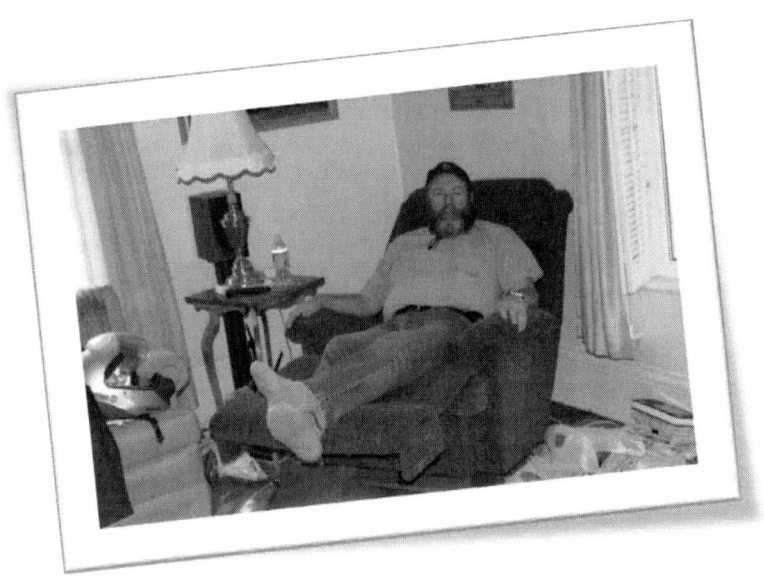

Dave in Nappanee

Day 11

January 12th 2008
From Nappanee Ontario to Joliette Quebec

I got up late because I knew I was only four to five hours from Joliette. We had coffee and cookies (Freshly baked by Dave's wife), and spent some times chatting again! Dave is a truck driver and has great advice about the road and places to stop at along the way. He also has an incredible sense of humour. Quick and witty! He can also imitate the people in the stories he tells. I laughed so hard, the back of my head was hurting. Even though I was in no hurry, I knew I had to leave as daylight ran out early; and the last thing I wanted to do was to go across Montreal on a motorcycle with a sidecar in the dark. It would be safer to play Russian roulette. So I packed Frosty, gave hugs and said my goodbyes and I was on my way.

Hwy 401 is not exactly a motorcycle friendly slab. It is fast and filled with angry Ontarians. It is also the main road for truckers in south eastern Canada.

401 turns into 40 in Quebec and this road is just like Indy 500; but with less curves. Speed limits are around 80 to 100 km/h and actual traffic speed over around 120 to "Who gives a shit!" it is absolutely nuts.

If you have to drive there, make sure you know where you are going, because tailgating at high speed with cars that are merging in or merging out is common place. And the room they leave between their bumpers and yours could MAYBE hold a pack of smoke or a package of Tums Anti-acid.

My dad often said to slow drivers while driving this road; "If you do not know where you are going-why are you going?" I made it through alive.

It was diner time when I rolled in Joliette. My brother Bruno, his wife Josee, my nephew Patrick and my niece Stephanie were there in the garage as the door opened and brought Frosty in. Making it to Joliette was another important step for me. Just like last year; I felt I had gone through another major step in this trip. The safety of knowing that if for any reasons I chose to quit, I would be with my family was somehow reassuring. Everything would be ok. I would have a place to leave Frosty and all my gear! I guess it is just a mental thing! All the people who have opened their homes to me during this trip, have told me the same thing, and assured me that I could leave my stuff in their homes if I chose to call it quit.

Joliette Quebec

Diner was waiting, and if you remember what I said last year about French Canadian cuisine; one thing comes to mind. "Artery clogging-belt stretching-stomach inflating-heart beat slowing-liver busting-bladder filling-mind numbing food!" And it was there waiting for me. Damn! The only thing better than this, is making love while eating this. No! Hold on a second? It is eating this while having sex. Yeah!!! That is it! Ok! Moving on!!!!

I did not know how long I would be in Joliette, but I told Bruno not more than two days. This was not a vacation. It was a stop where I would refill on my energy to attack the part that worried me the most. Eastern Quebec, then LABRADOR! Just pronouncing it gave me shivers.

Last year Newfoundland was THE major part; but this year Labrador was the one. I knew Newfoundland and Labrador are in the same area. But to me, they are separate. Labrador played with my mind more than

Newfoundland did! After a great evening spent catching up with my family and reassuring my mom that I would not do this again; I went to bed and asked not be woken till I woke up by myself, by either the sound of my own snoring or that gurgling/choking feeling as I breathed in the snot I drooled on my pillow because all the muscle in my jaw relaxed to the point where the only thing jiggling more is a bowl of Jell-O on a tread master. It was ten when I woke up and when I did; I looked outside as usual. What I saw was not exactly what I wanted to see.

Blowing snow and howling winds made the scenery look like Hum Well! Winter!! I think I could blame that one on the date. January 13th. I was still hoping it would clear enough for me to plough on through. But it stayed like this all day. They had already broken all the snow accumulation records they had; and looking at the high snow banks, I was sure it would get worse.

I wanted to go see my cousin Johanne! I am sure we all have a cousin or a family member we share a deep affinity with. Her and I have always connected and enjoyed each other. Our family know that if we were not cousins we would be together. Now hold on your horses here Sin crème! Take it easy here! Focus! Focus! Stay with me ok?

I always look forward to see her. When I showed up at her door for diner she gave me a big hug. We had dinner and stayed up late. We always have a few months or sometimes a year to catch up to. One of the reasons why we connect like this is that our relationship is not only written by the writings of time; but also by deep scars in our hearts caused by traumatic events in our lives. Loss is a word we do not only understand, but lived too many times. Allow me to explain! Let's go back to that fateful day!

It is the summer of 1965 and I am outside playing with my brother Bruno and Ginette. I am five years-old, and they both are three years-old. I loved Honey Combs cereal when I was a kid and so did they.

We each have a bowl in our hands and are snacking. We are across the street at my brother's friend place, and our bowls are now empty. A great idea comes to life in my mind.
"You have to know that I was a very chubby as a kid, and the only way for me to win a race against my svelte brother and cousin would be to cheat at the starting time"
I look at them and say *"The last one to get across the street to fill his bowl is a chicken!"*
And I start running before I finish saying it. My ability to accelerate is about the same as an overloaded semi. We lived a in a rural area where everyone knew everyone and traffic was (Almost) non- existent. It was a safe and quiet community. As I start running, Ginette catches up to me pretty much immediately, and as we both reach the edge of the road, Mr Lavallée; a friend of the family is coming down the road in his 1963 Meteor.

Because of a cedar hedge that is blocking his view and ours, we cannot see each other. So right there in front of me, less than a foot away; Ginette gets hit by the car. *43 years later I still can see it.* He hit the brakes and her little body gets thrown about eighty feet and hits a birch tree. I run to her and crawl on the ground besides her and call her name. But no answer! Not a sound! I am 5 years old-remember? As I say "Ginette! Ginette!" I gently take her head in my hand as I hold her shoulder and turn her face toward mine. She has no face left. I cannot understand what I am looking at. I do not know what it is. I gently put her little head down on the ground and start walking to my house where my mom who is babysitting Ginette for a few days is unaware of what has just taken place.
By now the neighbours are running outside to the scene of the accident. Mr Lavallée is crying holding Ginette, my brother is just standing there not knowing what is going on either, still as a post. I sit on the front porch and the sounds of my cries and the commotion outside get my mom to come outside. She sees me cry and asks me what is wrong. And as she is asking this, out of the corner of her eyes a little red, yellow and white dress at

the base of the tree catches her eyes. And then all hell breaks loose.

I never forgot this. And for years; I saw it happening in my mind time after time. Ginette would be 46 today. 2 years younger than her sister Johanne. My cousin!

I guess you could say that what Johanne and I have is something bigger than family. I ached for three decades because of this, and through it all Ginette's big sister always tried to help me understand that it was not my fault; even thought she did not know how it really happened. It was only a few years ago that I took her to the house and walked her on the street by the place where Ginette died and explained to her in details what happened. She needed to know and I needed to tell her.

.

This event is another one amongst so many that has taught me life is too short, and that if you shouldn't waste the precious seconds, minutes, hours, days given to you to live, f$#@%ing around hesitating about whether or not you should do something your heart is telling you to do. Once lost; this time is gone! To never be given again. You will NEVER get it back. So here we have it!

I left Johanne's place at midnight and went to my brother's place. Slept like a baby right through the night. The next day was spent with my mom and brother. After two days in Joliette, and watching the weather channel; I found out that a huge cold front was about to hit Eastern Quebec, and that timing would be crucial. I decided to leave on the 15th. Tomorrow! My family and friends said the same thing too. Meanwhile people were logging on my website, and letting me know about the weather which is just about to crap out. (Great minds think alike) Leaving that day was a good idea!

While I was in Joliette, a radio station from Florida contacted me and asked me if I would mind giving them an interview now and one when I came back. *"Sure! If I make it out of there!"* The radio interviewer and I laughed about it, but inside I knew that the fear about the TLH was very real and building up. There is something about this destination that rattled the deepest parts of me and made me wonder if what I was about to tackle was actually not about to become my last mistake. Lately I had started to compare the topography and isolation I had experienced when I did it in summer, to what it might be in winter.

The voices of people who live there and who have told me to not attempt this were still ringing in my mind! The naysayers' voices were not bothering me. But these folks are not naysayers! They live there, and what is to me an adventure, is at the same time a part of the country they know, respect, and fear equally. The TLH constabulary had also told me that it was NOT a good idea.

Still! The little voice in me that has always guided me was telling me to move forward. I chose to believe it when I left over two weeks ago, but it was sometimes muffled by the sound of fear and doubt.

I talked to my brother about it, and even though we were raised by a fearless father who loved life and taught us things like how to dive off a 70 feet bridge into a narrow gorge; even Bruno was wondering if this was not pushing it too far. That night when I went to bed I prayed and asked dad for guidance.

The voice I heard was the same I heard coming out of his mouth when he was here with us. "Go Paul! Go!"

So lying in bed that night I chose to go forward and ignore this little unknown voice inside of me.

I have said many times to whoever wanted to hear me that I believe that when it is your time to go; you will go!

Sometimes (Like today) it is easier said than done. I suppose it is a natural reaction to stop in your tracks and listen to the sound of fear. After all, it is the sound of doubts and the unknown! Fear is believed by many; including me, to be a healthy and necessary emotion. Some may argue that, but it is how we were raised, and how I understand it. We were taught that fear happens and that when it does, we should ask ourselves why it is happening.

Laying in my bed tonight I think of all I have lost. I am not being gloomy here, but sometimes thinking of all you have lost helps you realize that what you have lost is really a gain cut short. Your life is richer for having had it than it would have been without. Tonight as I focus on this I realize that I would rather go doing what I like and have no regrets; than just succumb to fear and lose the chance to live through what I have set out to accomplish.

That night my last words before I went to sleep were *"Screw you fear! I am too busy living!"*

Good night!

Day 14

January 15th 2008
Leaving Joliette Québec toward the TLH

Sunrise as I leave Joliette

It was 6:00 AM when I woke up. The plan was for Bruno to follow me and film me as I rolled out of town. We would travel together to Trois-Rivieres where he works; and have breakfast at a restaurant then part our ways. As I walked outside it was as expected.-15° C and lots of snow. It looked like Labrador could be waiting for me with a grin on its cold white face. He had my camera and captured videos as he drove. He was enjoying this like a little kid. Bruno was always the mature one! He got married young, went to university, enrolled in the forces as an engineer and raised two kids. Doing things like this for him have always been a dream, but the reality of his life do not allow him to do it; at least not in an immediate future!

As a dad he cannot and should not, but he has always enjoyed watching his big brother living his life a he pleased; following his own rules and making his own tracks. The St-Lawrence was looking asleep under this white cover.

Bruno filming me as we go

The farmlands on both shores were covered by a white blanket. It is hard to imagine looking at them now, that in a few months they will be filled with the lush colors of bountiful crops.

We got to Trois-Rivieres and went to the restaurant not too far from Bruno's work. When we got there people looking out the windows couldn't believe what they were looking at as I came in and made a perfect controlled slide, and donut then parked in front of them. Showing off? Perhaps! Was I proud to be out there enjoying something people believe cannot be enjoyed at this time of the year? You bet your ass I was!

While we were eating sitting by the window, two police officers from the Sureté du Québec drove in. They got out of their cruiser and stopped to look at Frosty. They saw the plate, smiled and walked in. As they walked by me one of them says *"This is absolutely crazy! But damn it looks like a lot of fun!"* After telling him where I was going he shook my hand, wished me luck and moved on.

We finished our breakfast and left. I hugged my brother as he took a couple pictures of his crazy brother; and we each went on our way. Love you Bedo!

The St-Lawrence River behind the Frozen Quebec countryside

The drive from Trois-Rivieres to Quebec City was smooth. Mighty cold, but smooth! Autoroute 40 is almost 200 kilometres to Quebec City, and every single vehicle that drove by me slowed down as the occupants looked wondering *"What the hell? "*

Some took pictures, some gave me the thumbs up, and others just smiled and moved on. I decided to stop in Donnacona for fuel and a coffee. As I made my way to the fuel pump a Sureté du Quebec cruiser pulled behind me. A young female officer comes out and tells me that she HAS to ask me for my papers as she does not know what to make of my personalized plate. She said she has a trainee with her and would like to show her how it is done. I told her I would give her my papers as soon as I was done fuelling. Meanwhile she asked me where I was going and all the other usual questions. Once I was done fuelling I handed her my papers and one of my cards; and asked her to check it out. She said she is a motorcyclist herself and that she would. She looked at my stuff, wished me good luck and left. It turns out that she would later log on to my site and chat a bit with me as she followed my progress.

This trip, like the one last year made me realize how much I need the brightness of the sun and the light. Victoria is beautiful; but it is so grey in winter that it brings you down. I am affected by S.A.D. Seasonal Affective Disorder like many Canadians, and the clear blue skies and blinding white snow reminded me how invigorating white winters can be.

For a couple of hours I rode along the frozen St-Lawrence. It was quiet and peaceful. I made it to Quebec City and went on eastward on 40. The ice over the St-Lawrence has broken into huge pieces and these pieces are frozen together like one big mean jagged puzzle.

Perfect and challenging for the Traversee du Fleuve! It is an event where people race across the St-Lawrence in whalers. Rowing, hauling, pushing, dragging, lifting, and carrying their vessel as fast as they can against other teams from all over the world. The Quebec/Canadian team is always hard if not impossible to beat in this event.

As I ride, little towns appear and disappear alongside this frozen landscape, like L'ange Gardien (Guardian Angel) Château Richer, St-Anne de Beaupré. St-Pétronille, St-Fereole des Neiges, St-Tite des Caps etc. Most names in Québec start with St, Saint, Ste.

A strong reminder of the once powerful Catholic influence over this land! The names are pretty much the only thing that remains of this era when the church was either revered or feared. If you have a chance to travel through these parts you will see that all the villages and

The bridge for l'ile D'Orléans

towns no matter how small they are; have a huge (Often cathedral like) church. Driving down those country side roads and seeing the steeples appear in the distance announcing the quickly approaching community is an event that has been romanticized and written about by travellers from all over the world.
The ride was long, cold and slippery in many places. Especially when I hit La Malbaie where the changes in elevation would make the road go from dry, cold and clear, to icy and slippery in one short Holy Shit second.

La Malbaie! It is an area of Quebec that is visited by many during the summer and fall. I have always associated this part of the country to some part of Europe where valleys, mountains and farmland stretch

One of many places in La Malbaie

as far as the eye can see. Rolling hills and pasture along the St-Lawrence make for a place that post cards are made of.

I stopped in Baie St-Paul at????? Where else-but Tim's for coffee and soup. While I was in there I met with a fellow that had been following me on my site and lives right on the road I was travelling on through Baie St-Paul. He came in and we chatted about the trip and how he would love to do something like this. We exchanged info and went on my way.

I made to the La Traverse de Tadoussac. A little free ferry crossing that interrupts in a very nice way an otherwise constant hugging of the coast by Route 138.

Route 132 is on the south shore of the St-Lawrence and takes you to the Gaspé Peninsula where the legendary sea food is only matched by the world class scenery. You just don't want to do it in winter, especially on a bike as the roads which are awful at best in summer become a slalom course around potholes that have been known to break Semis' suspension components.

A little rest area on my way to Tadoussac

At one point I was going down the road and I started to smell something! It smelled sweet. Really freaking sweet! I was going *"Oh Shit! I am losing coolant!"* I stopped on the side of the road and couldn't find anything wrong. Nothing? Frosty's engine was dry! I thought it was something in the air. An hour later it was still smelling like this! I stopped again, and I smelled the exhaust to see if I was burning coolant! A head gasket maybe? Nope! What the hell!???? I kept going and then I stopped to take a picture. I opened my tank bag and smoke poured out of it. What the %$#&!

What started out as a good idea almost cost me three thousand dollars of video equipment and my family jewels. OUCH!
I got my cameras out, and the towel sitting at the bottom of my tank bag was burning and smoking.
I threw it in the snow and looked at my stuff to make sure nothing was damaged. The Oxford Wrap around heated grips I was using as a tank bag warmer to keep

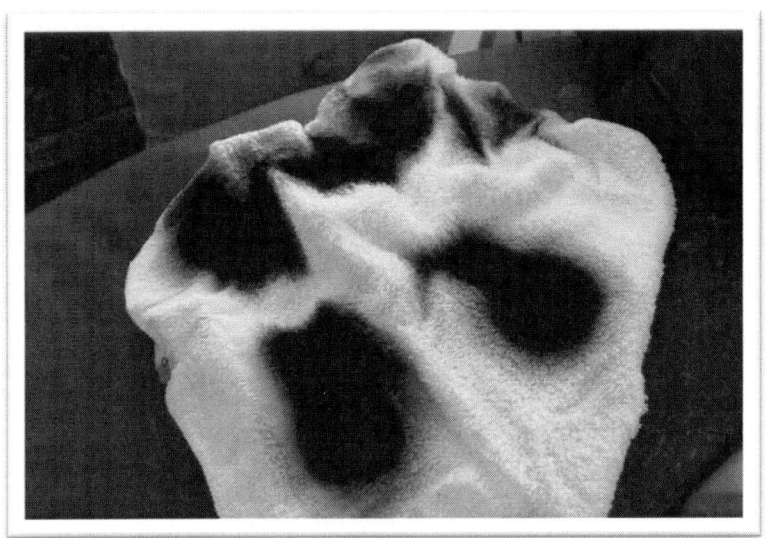

My tank bag warmer/ nut burner

The black marks are burn marks

my video equipment warm and working well had heated so much that it set the towel and foam pad on fire.
My ear plugs case was melted to crap, my liner keeping the cameras from direct contact with the grips was melted, and part of the wire for the digital camera battery pack had also melted a bit. I was cussing, I was swearing, and I invented some more swears. Cussing is in English! Swearing is in French!
St Eucharistie de maudit Tabarnac de sœur blindée de colisse de sin crème d'apocalypse de chrisse de cinciboire d'arias d'cochonnerie d'esti de calver de patente de crisse sale de ciboire qu'est ce qui pense de faire des crisse de cochonneries de bébelles de même de sin crème que j'aimerais rencontrer la casse de bain qui a invente c't'esti de patente a gosse la! Sacrament!

In English? You do not want to know!!
Anyway! I cut off the part of the harness that had melted itself into a patch of dry crap and tossed it. I fixed what

was left of the cord. Kept the one that looked half baked and half-ass good, and wrapped it in what was left of the towel to make sure that it did not transfer flame thrower like heat like that again. *Shit man! I wanted heat! Not fire!* After all it is a pair of hand grips for motorcycles. Do not buy this? If this was to happen to your hands you would not need to go for breakfast. Just peel your now crispy hands off the bars! Son of a B....that hurts- then put them in the snow to make sure they bubble nicely; then pour Aunt Jemima syrup on them and voila! Enjoy! A quick modern breakfast filled with protein! Hmmmm good!

Anyway after bringing down from heaven all the saints with my swearing and kicking them back up; I put this big pile of swears in the same pile from yesterday. I guess you could say I am racking up credits for hell. Let me explain! Yesterday as I was on my way to visit my cousin when I noticed the side zippers on my Arctic suit had split!

I proceeded to create another two pages of custom swears. It probably hooked on something while I was in the garage and screwed it up. It is now sewn shut and if it breaks-well-I will need another zipper. If shit like this keeps happening I will have enough custom swears to write a book. " How to embarrass Satan, and scare the hell out of Catholicism" in two volume, by Paul Mondor.

Anyway! I made it to the Tadoussac ferry. I have always loved this part of the trip on the north shore of the St-Lawrence. It was great. The ice was running, the wind was blowing and I was taking pictures while everyone was stuck in their cars looking at me like I was crazy! I might be, but I was having fun! How about you in your minivan with your diaper filling machines and the wife that will not even look at you anymore because she wanted to stop for coffee but could not because you told "A bit later Hunny" this bit later buddy will get you on the couch with Fido!

Little rest area near Tadoussac

An icy parking lot near the ferry made for a perfect evening picture

As I am taking pictures a guy comes to me and says "Shit man! You speak French?" Yep! Then he goes on asking me where I was coming from and where I was going. I was thinking *"You are parked three micro inch from my plate you nimrod! That is why you can't see my plate!"* I do not know why but I instantly disliked him. I said "Victoria BC and Goose Bay Labrador!"
"No Way! You shitting me aren't you?"
"Nope!"
"You cannot! This bike would not haul this side buggy, (That is what he said I swear) *that far and that long? Not big enough and you cannot ride this long in winter! I know I ride side buggy and I know I thing or two about them!"*

Frozen pier in Tadoussac. Swim anyone???

I was thinking *"Really! Is that why you are driving a Sonata with Adolphine Hitler next to you?"* (She made Hitler look happy!)
"You ride sidecars?"
"Yep! Been for years! And I can tell you that your rig is not set up properly just looking at it!"

I thought *"Really!"* Hmmmmmmm! Hold on Let me take off my fucking helmet here, I want to show you something-you moron! No! Let's see if you are set up for a swim"
But I did not!

Can you spot Frosty on the Tadoussac ferry? She was hiding

I just said *"That is ok buddy! It works for me and has for close to 7000 kms now"* and walked away looking like I had something urgent to do. Like getting the hell away from him! Something like thinking and wondering if anyone would see me; if I threw him overboard? Naaah!

Anyway the crossing was beautiful and perfect. The only thing that would have made it better was if I had found out whether or not Mr.Sidebuggy could swim. Just kidding! Not! Ok! Letting go!

**The Tadoussac Ferry
coming across the St-Lawrence**

I made it to Escoumains at the Pelchat Hotel complex where I signed in for the night. Right outside my window were about a dozen pickup trucks with trailers, and on the other side were about 40 snowmobiles. How cool was that? I contacted Rene in Baie-Comeau and told him I would be there the following day. I could have made it to Baie-Comeau that night, but I felt like stopping and resting.

It will be a short day tomorrow! I will stop at his place and leave for Labrador the following day. I have talked to a couple of truckers in gas stations on my way down here, and they told me that the TLH was looking good! Lots and lots of snow and colder than usual; but the road was well graded. Looking at all these snowmobiles in here that night I was thinking that if I could find a place where I could rent one, I would go snowmobiling in Goose Bay.
But I was getting ahead of myself here. I was better off worrying whether or not I would make it to Goose Bay.

At the rate I was going I thought I would be in GB in about 3-4 days. That is if I did not burn myself to a freaking crisp before!
Has anyone thought about how close to my nuts the base of this tank bag really was? I am digressing here!

I grabbed a sauna that night and jumped in the hot tub for a bit. Sitting there with steam all around me, it was easy to forget it was -20°C out there.
I went back to my room after that, updated my notes and blog and hot the hay.

Good night

Day 15

Escoumains Quebec
January 16, 2008
5500 kilometres later

Outside Motel Pelchat in les Escoumains Quebec

Got up this morning at six and walked outside. It was no sauna or hot tub. Mommy!!!
The sky was crystal clear and stars were like-right in my face. The air was beautifully crisp! Hey! Self-talk helps you know? I decided to go back to bed as I would be at Los Tabarnacos (Rene Roy) early today. So there was no rush. I went back to bed. Got up at eight and was ready to go. Sleeping in felt good! After packing Frosty and suiting up while she was warming up, I took off. The road in these parts is really nice scenery wise, but the surface is like going through an exploded mine field. Heaves, cracks, potholes and all sorts of good stuff that made me say "Thanks I put an Ohlin's shock on the back and upgraded the front suspension and the sidecar shock, otherwise; my kidneys would have been turned into soup.

Previous pages: Pictures taken along the way from les Escoumains to Baie-Comeau. The ice was running and the sun bouncing on it made the St-Lawrence look like a giant mirror. It was another of these times that made motorcycling in winter all worth while

At this time of the year everything is frozen and looks like a post card. I absolutely loved it. As I made my way to Baie-Comeau I stopped many times. That is why I got there at twelve.

There are so many pictures opportunities, and you just can't take advantage of them all. When I got to Baie-Comeau I stopped for coffee, and while I was there, one of Lost Tabarnacos friends, Real Murray, whom I had never met-stopped by with his daughter and chatted for a while. He said he had phoned Rene to let him know I was here! Small town folks! I LOVE IT! Everyone knows everyone and they care! Then Rene got there showed up shortly after. And as I was about to bite into my Tim's sandwich he said that his wife Dianne had prepared lunch René and I. I doggy bagged the thing and we scooted to his house!

Let me tell you this. We had a hell of great meal! Meat, cream, cheese, rice, gravy, sauce, spuds- this is the stuff that sticks to your ribs and helps you keep on going. Good...Great.....Freaking fantastic! Yeah! That's it! Thanks Diane!

(Here you go ZZRon! Foood!) It was so damn good that it could have brought a dead man back to life! This was like an orgasm for the taste buds!! Don't get me wrong I love the sandwiches and soup I normally eat when I am on the road, but comparing that to Dianne's food would be like trying to compare Julia Roberts to the Queen when she gets up in the morning! Whhoaahh!
Rene! How come you don't weigh 500 lbs with food like this? Come on fess up! How come? Oh-Sorry! You are right! Can't put that in writing!

Rene (Los Tabarnacos) doing what he likes. Coordinating my trip up the TLH and being damn good at it. He has given me many good tips and contacts for the ride. Thank you René

This was the first time I met Rene and his wife. It felt like I had known him a long time. An avid motorcyclist, a great host, and a heart as big as the St-Lawrence! Thanks Rene!
We spent part of the evening chatting and shooting crap and the most important part; burping Dianne's dinner. I wondered all night if I could ask for second, you know- evening snack-but I couldn't do it. Rene and I looked for roads conditions and forecasts on the net and tried to get me an idea of what it would be like. Rene knows a few guys who regularly travel on the TLH and had already done his homework. They told him that the TLH had been cleared a bit wider than normally because they were expecting some Heavy haulers delivering some heavy equipment to the Fire Lake mine in Fremont.

This could be good news and bad news. Good news was that they kept the road clear as much as they weather allowed them. The bad news was that there would be some big freaking trucks with some bigger freaking machines on their trailers just waiting for me to com e around a bend and become an "On the fly grease job"

He also pointed me to a few spots where I could seek shelter if needed as well as gas locations. In the past months before the trip he also alerted the TLH constabulary and they knew I was coming. They had emailed me and told me so as well. It also looked like all the truckers knew already that I would be there; and knowing how it works; I was sure that they would radio my position to each other as often as they could.

We hung around and shot shit for the rest of the afternoon. Now here was the plan! I am leaving tomorrow morning around 7:30 to attack 389 toward Manicouagan 5 where I will turn east toward Fremont Quebec and Labrador City! I was hoping to make the 580 kms the next day! (I told you I smoke good shit!)
If I could not-I could stop at the Relais Gabriel which was before that. They rent rooms and cabins for hunters and fishermen, and the lady there told me to knock on

the door even if I got there at midnight; and that they would give me a cabin.

For the following day, the plan was to leave Labrador city and head to Goose Bay. For Friday afternoon! Hmmmm! We will see! On the way I wanted to stop in Churchill Falls as well because the local newspaper wanted to talk to me. There was also the magazine in Labrador City, and then the one in Goose Bay! If all went well; I would leave Goose Bay Saturday morning or Sunday morning and be back in Baie-Comeau for Sunday night or Monday night.

Then I would head to Joliette where I would spend a few days, and head back to Victoria.

I read this today, and it confirms that what I always doubted is in fact true. They did slap me on the head instead of on the ass when I was born. This would explain so much!

Notes from that night: I am reading my notes tonight I cannot help but think, or should I say-know, that what I was thinking about during the day is absolutely true. As a matter of act-every-damn day! It is that I would not be here today doing what I am doing and having fun at it, if it were not of the two most important things in my life. First! God's grace to give me this life, health and the taste for life I have.

And second! Melanie! I love her of course more than I can say in these pages. But make no mistake about it. Going back to her is what makes the return home feasible. Because I know what and whom I am going back to! I am having so much fun out here. And I am blessed to be out here! But I am even luckier for her. It is one thing to get carried away in this, and it is another to see past this. Here's to you Hunny! Here's to many miles, many years and many smiles like this together!

Good night!

Day 16

January 17th 2008
Baie-Comeau Quebec
Almost 5900 kilometres later

I got up in the morning and I was psyched! I was ready to hit the TLH to Goose Bay! I had to leave right there and then before I changed my mind. And the temperature outside was not helping.
It was -28°C! I wanted cold-I got cold!!
I asked for it-I had it-and shut up I would! While I was sleeping Rene went to Tim's and got us some coffee. What a way to start a day! We left, and then stopped at the Shell station to fuel up Frosty. Rene told me that a friend of his who lives not too far from the Manic 2 Power Dam wanted to meet me and take some pictures before I headed north.

The start of a 2200 km trip starting at -38C.

Rene and I stopped at the beginning of the TLH outside Baie-Comeau and took a picture of me at the sign Picture. The sign kind of said it all and to be honest here scared the crap out of me.

Manicouagan II
Just 28 kilometres into it and already -38C! I look at this picture and I still feel the way I felt that morning. Completely out of place!

Standing in front of the sign announcing what I was to tackle I realized how big what I was embarking on was. Actually for a few short minutes (Very short) I felt like I was out of my mind. Looking back at this I realized that no matter how much I had prepared, I was not prepared for what laid ahead.

After taking pictures and videos, we shook hands and I told Rene *"See you in a week!"* He said *"Be careful Paul! Be very careful ok?"* and I took off. Within minutes it was obvious that I had made the right call by bringing survival gear and extra fuel. Without these on this road, breaking down in the middle of nowhere means that in no time (Minutes) you are a goner. What was asphalt covered with sand quickly turned into sheer ice covered with snow. I am told that because of environmental reasons, salt is not used in these parts, and they only use sand in hills for obvious safety reasons. Suddenly the TLH had a face! It was big! It was icy and it was cold!

The sight of the dams was really sobering. It reminded me again how small and insignificant I was amongst those huge immobile structures just standing there defying the cold and the forces of nature.

It is hard to explain how I felt being on this road. Starting right away at -38C, and knowing that I would have to do 2200 kms of it before I could get back on asphalt again was something I thought I was prepared for, but truly was not. This road is rough beyond belief.

The sight of Frosty in front of Manic 2, the smoke coming out of her exhaust and the crispy sound of the snow and ice as she rides on this surface showed ne in no uncertain way that this was the REAL SHIT. *This wasn't something to F%$#@ around with!*

There are no words I can write that can describe how I felt as I walked along this amazing site. A 600 feet long, 60 feet high wall of ice. Water pouring out of the cliff had frozen on contact with air. The size and beauty of it made frosty and I look like ants.

Manicouagan 5

I remember when my dad took us there when I was about 12. We stood on top and looked down. We could see a school bus at the bottom and it looked like a baby ant.
This was for many years Canada's biggest and most powerful power dam. Still is a colossus in the world of power dam.
After a couple of curves it was obvious that the front tire was not going to cut it without studs. So in my infinite wisdom I decided to install them. But I would have to wait to find a spot on the side of the road where I could pull over and install them. The last thing I wanted was to stand on the side of the road and then "Bam". I could almost see it in my mind. The truck driver just coming down the road after a long cold day and suddenly; Kah-Klonk! What was that?"
But the "Right moment" came quicker than planned because, shortly after that I was going down a right hand turn and lost traction. The front end just kept going. Holy shit! Whhooaaaaaahh! I stayed on the throttle when I realized there was nothing coming

toward me. I swung the rig's rear end left as I hard as I could-it was easy with my ass sucking the seat right up-and slammed perfectly on the snow bank and rode alongside just like if I was on bobsled run.

I think I popped a vein in my ass. I tried to keep her from climbing up and eject me like a rock in a sling shot. We bounced off the snow bank and then both wheels on the bike got back on the shoulder (at road level) and rode back on my side. I am not sure but I heard that later that day drivers were driving by and wondering what was that brown line going from one side of the road, up the snow bank and back on the road.

The TLH is gravel in summer. In winter it is ice and ice only. The road surface is grooved by grader blades and the surface is rougher than anything I have ever seen. It is bone-crushing!

I tried to steer her with the hack's brake but-no! No-Go! It is just a freaking miracle I did not crash. I stopped on the side and calmed down a bit. By this time it was getting dark, and there was no way I would make it if I do not change the way I rode. *"Shit! I am only 50 clicks and still have over 2100 of this to go?? It is going to be insanely hard to stay up or alive on this road!"* I almost turned around. My back was hurting, my arms were throbbing and my nerves were being tested in a way I had not expected. But I was having fun!! I know I am weird. I took a 10 minute break parked there on the side of the road, and no one went by during this time. Sorry to say this, but you hit the ditch down there at this time of the year, and if you are hurt and have no way to reach anyone; you will die of hypothermia in a hell of a hurry! Most likely you will come out of Booboo's ass in the spring! Again! The thought of how much more dangerous than the great lakes in that snow storm this was going to be could not get out of my mind

"Focus Dammit! Focus Paul! "You either do this or you shot the hell up and turn around!" were the words I said out loud on my helmet. As you know talking to myself works!

This place I was in was not the place to lose the battle against fear. I knew they were forecasting snow in these parts, but with no significant accumulation; but forecasting weather in Labrador is about as reliable as a Crack head you just sent to make your night bank deposit.

Anyway! I decided to move on. But before I did, I wanted to install the studs on the front wheel. By now the temperature was still around -35°C and the sun was disappearing quickly.

I didn't have much time to do this, and there was only one way to do this, and it was the right way. I opened the hack's cover and took the jack out to lift the front end of the rig so I could spin the front wheel as I installed the studs. I knew I couldn't hold the studs with my gloved hands to put them in the drill bit. I had to remove my gloves. Once I had laid out my tools and that the studs' container was opened I removed my gloves and I put the few studs on.

It took about thirty seconds for me to put one stud and my fingers were already numb. I couldn't do it! I was

already hurting. I stopped, put my gloves back on and put my hands on the muffler tip and moved my fingers rapidly inside the gloves.
My gloves were already as cold inside as it was outside. My fingers were already tingling and I knew this was not good! I jumped on the bike and took off.
After a couple minutes I could barely feel my fingers and had trouble handling Frosty. Shit!
I had to thaw out now! It was obvious that the heated grips and my hands inside the Hippo hands® wouldn't be enough. So I stopped, jumped off the bike, opened the sidecar cover and got the propane tank out, and connected the heater to it. My hands were now stinging and I could not feel my fingertips anymore.
I could hardly hold the lighter, let alone light it up. Why the hell didn't I buy one of these battery operated BBQ lighter instead? Wouldn't have worked anyway! It was cold enough to freeze the balls off a brass monkey, so it would have killed those little AAA batteries in a hurry.

I would have loved to see the Energizer® Bunny scoot by playing its stupid little drum at these temperatures. I would have grabbed him and stuffed my hands up his ass to warm up! Here-take this you annoying little shit!

I knew damn well I had no choice, so I took my glove off and lit the Bic® lighter. It felt like I was grinding my finger off on bench grinder. It took me all I had, and then I heard this amazing sound! Poof! The flame was on! I took the tarp Rene had given me, wrapped myself in it, and squatted over the heater. If someone had come by I am sure I would have looked like a really weird Teepee. Within then minutes I got warm enough to remove my gloves and thaw my hands and fingers off over the heater. I will always be thankful for this Coleman heater. It turns out it will save my life more than once!
When my hands felt better and my fingers stopped tingling; I put my gloves back on, put my shit away, and sat back on Frosty. I put my hands in the Hippo hands® and told Frosty "Tabarnac que ca passer proche! Shit

that was close! I looked at the sidecar and said *"Thanks!"* did I say how happy I was that I brought that damn hack? Well hear me again Dammit! I was happy! It was the second time in half an hour it had saved my ass. I would not swear at it for the rest of the trip.

As I was just about to take off, a Hydro Quebec truck slowly went by and the driver asked as he was waving- *'Are you ok?"* I gave him the nod, he gave me the smile and thumb up we both took off!

This first part of the road leading to manic 5 was obviously wicked. The road got rougher just like René had told me. It was (dam) rough! ☺
I would find out shortly enough that this was nothing compared to what it would be like later. We will come to that later! I scooted along and made it to the fuel stop where I also fuelled up on coffee and soup. I was told that this was one of the only two stops between Baie-Comeau and the Quebec-Labrador border, and that the food was good.
It was a $12.00 Bla-meal! So Bla that I started drooling of boredom in my helmet later trying to remember what it tasted like! Then I remembered! Cardboard! That is it! Cardboard! I had just eaten $12.00 worth of cardboard.

At least my crapped would be wrapped. But the people I met there were great and we had a good time. Everyone from the waitress to the cook and the Hydro Quebec guys were great, so it made up for the cardboard food.
As I was about to leave the parking lot, a trucker was just rolling in and waved at me to stop. I stopped by his door and he was on the CB radio telling someone *"He is just besides me! You won't believe this shit!"* It turns out that all the truckers were aware of my presence and were radioing my position as they met me on the road. *How cool is that??*
As I got further north east, it got colder by the mile. I knew how cold it was just by looking at the rigs I came across; as the white thick smoke coming out of their stacks was a dead giveaway.

Frosty was also pushing white smoke out of her exhaust. She was working hard but was running just fine. Good girl!

I kept on going and made it to Relais Gabriel for fuel and coffee. But before I walked in I stopped on the edge of the parking lot to lube Frosty's chain. I jacked her up and lubed the chain real well. The chain and sprockets were taking a beating with this relentless hammering. Right next to me was a large shed with machinery parked outside.

This is my breath freezing coming out of my helmet. I have to say that if you are going to ride in cold, this helmet is the one to wear.

A couple guys came walking and said Tabarnac! Quesse tu fa icitte? Es-tu fou colisse? What the F%$#@ are you doing here? Are you F%$#@ nuts? We chatted as I put my tools away and they invited me in for coffee. They wanted to take a picture of me because they were saying that their buddies would not believe them unless they had a picture of this crazy French Canadian! I fuelled up and went in. In temperatures sticking around the -30ºC mark all day, Frosty's MPG dropped down quite a bit. I guess the hack didn't help either.

They were the guys who cleared the road over winter. They were from Newfoundland. The island they were spending the winter there away from their family, working.

One of them said that they were waiting to hear from the Fire Lake mine about a job they were suppose to get operating the big monster dump trucks. Money was supposed to be much better and they could see their family more often. Doing a job in isolated area has always been something I wanted to do.

I guess I can see myself sitting around the wood stove after a long day of work, sipping on coffee and watching the snow fall down. But to them it was not as romantic as I saw it. After about an hour and promising them that I would stop on my way back; I took off again. By then it was darker outside and I probably had just another half hour of daylight at most.

I was not sure what I was doing and why! I could have stayed at the Relais Gabriel, enjoy a nice relaxing night in a cabin and take off the day after.

But something wanted me to ride at night. So I did! Night riding on the TLH in winter on a motorcycle gives new meaning to the words "Fear" and "Stress"

I have always loved to ride at night. I know deer and all the objects you cannot see are out there, but somehow I love it. On the island here, I take off to go to Long Beach, which is a 700 kms (430 miles or so) at around 11:00 PM. I ride all night at a relaxed pace as I have the road to myself and stop here and there to have a coffee or hot chocolate (I bring my thermos) on the side of the road and enjoy the stars. The peace and quiet that I experience riding at night is therapeutic (Pretty good for a Frenchman). I took a couple of friends on one of these night run with me this summer as they wanted to it, but with someone they know is used to this. And they absolutely loved it. Victor Sanchez and Taher Al Tayeb now know what it is to ride all night, watch the stars, have a good breakfast, and come back home to a bed that will just be so comfy.

I took off again and hoped I would make it to Fremont or Labrador City tonight. I couldn't help but think that I should have stopped at the Relais. After a couple of minutes the sun setting on the horizon and the scenery changing to dark clothes kept my mind busy enough to stop worrying about the 'what if's'.

The sun was going down on the TLH. My first time on the TLH in winter and I was about to ride in the dark

It is 270 clicks from Relais Gabriel to Fremont and another 28 to Labrador city. By the time I hit the mile marker 430 something it was pitch black out there.

The wind was blowing like hell but at least it was a tail wind. The thing with that was that it dropped some fresh snow on the road and the road became like a skating rink. High pucker factor of about 8.1! Before I knew it I was reliving the Sault St-Marie-Trans Canada Highway shutdown all over again! But this time X 10.
The last 3 hours to Fremont/ Labrador City were really making me push my limits like I had ever done before. e. It felt like I was force feeding myself new info every

second that forced me to learn something new and improve my skills..

There was no time for practice and even less for forgiveness. The first try had to be the right one. No second chance. This made my stomach literally hurt with tension. It was dark and it was more slippery than anything else I had ever ridden on. I did not know the road, and couldn't rely on any past experience. Wouldn't have mattered anyway because nothing compares to this shit! It was "Adapt now! Or die trying!"

At one point in the last 90 clicks before Fremont I saw three eighteen wheelers in the ditch. Seeing them appear in the dark was like seeing ghost ships slowly emerging out of a fog bank. Every slow passing second was exposing more of the rigs' lines and shapes covered by snow. It was eerie and kind of sobering in a weird beautiful way at the same time.

Mother Nature was slowly covering them just like a Python slowly swallowing its prey. Under this thick layer of snow they looked look more some weird monsters sleeping in the snow than trucks.

This snow was so deep; it looked as if the rigs just sunk in it like flour. There was so much snow everywhere I was thinking *"Shit this stuff must be here till August!"*

A few times I came across some rigs and even though they slowed down when they saw me the snow their wheels were stirring up blinded me as they passed! This is fine if the roads is straight, but believe me it is not!

The last sign I saw said " Narrow road for 115 kms Caution". I finally made it to Fremont (The wall), the last city in the province of Quebec. Their winters are so cold and windy that this mining town decided to build this seven storey- three quarter of a mile long building to protect the city from the winds.

In this building you can find everything this community needs. From a hotel to restaurants and hairdressers, to bowling alleys and grocery stores.

Even the entrances are built at a 45 angle from the wall so the wind does not have a grip on them. You can read more about it at this site.
http://www.duplessis-travelguide.com/Caniapiscau/Fermont-windbreak-wall/
I stopped for fuel and called it a night. Even if Labrador city was only 28 kms away I couldn't go any further.

When I got there, all I wanted to do was sleep. I was absolutely bagged. That road was so rough, it is hard to describe. Poor visibility combined with snow banks blending together with road and the thought that if I got off in the ditch no one would find me till spring, made this day an exhausting one.
When I pulled over at the hotel entrance I instantly became an attraction. I was too tired to care though! Shit was I ever bagged! This town is built by Fire Lake mine.

This ice road is so hard and rough I cannot even explain it.

Cold here is not only a word; it is a way of living. It is respected; it is feared and taken seriously. You do not venture out here not knowing how to handle what she can throw at you. As I signed up for my room I struck a conversation with the young lady at the counter.

She was another reason why I believe that French Canadian women are the most beautiful women in the world. She was breath taking to say the least. She was very quick to remind me that being here on a motorcycle at this time of the year was a bad idea.

The 6 foot 3-300 pounds miner standing next to me was also quick to agree with her. I was in the wall, staring at a human wall.

This visit looked promising! I went outside and unpacked Frosty. I unloaded the most valuable things I had as I would be on the third floor and would not have her in sight. Something was telling that these people were honest and I somehow felt safe around them.

Plus they were forecasting -45°C tonight and didn't want to leave my photo/video equipment outside in that cold.

I walked upstairs and jumped in the shower right after I unpacked my frozen laptop. I wanted to write some notes about the day. That is if I was not getting a blue screen of death saying *"Are you out of your F%$#@ mind? You really think Windows can start after being frozen all day and bounced around like that? Man! Windows has issues in normal temperatures! Go back to bed your technically handicapped twit!"*

Fifteen minutes in the shower seemed to do the trick. Some of my parts were so shrivelled I am sure the Raisin Made® company would have mistaken it for one of their products.

When I got out of the shower I looked outside and it looked unreal. The snow was swirling against the building like waves hitting a sea wall. The parking lot was full of truck and pick-up trucks; and they were all plugged in. And Frosty was out there in this white nightmare and with only company the light shining off the lamp post in front of the hotel entrance.

I felt bad for her. I wished I could have brought her in. I am sure I could have if I had asked, but because of her new appendage (The sidecar) she wouldn't fit through the door. The last thought that hit my mind before I went to sleep was that I hoped she would start in the morning.

This was by very far the coldest we had seen, and according to what they were saying; a lot worse was just around the bend

Recap? The first day on the TLH turned out to be one of the hardest-let me take this back-the hardest ride I have ever been on.

Good night

Day 17

Friday morning January 18, 2008
Fremont Quebec
645 clicks since Baie-Comeau

It was about 7:00 AM and it was -38°C outside. I was ready to go! I packed my stuff, put it on the valet cart and went downstairs. Valet cart! That is funny just writing it. Sounds like the Bahamas!
When I got downstairs, the entrance way was packed with miners dressed like Eskimos.

Every day they wait there for the bus to take them to Fire Lake mine. As I walked towards them they parted a way for me to go through; just like the sea opened up for Moses when he led his people to the promise land. Except that this time, for me they are opening a passage for me to walk to my own version of a hole.. They looked at me in absolute shock and did not say a word.
They just nodded as to say "Hi" and remained silent. When I came back in after loading Frosty, one of them asked me where I was going. I said *"Goose Bay!"* he said *"Really? You know that this road is barely travelled in winter and that the reason for that is that it is too dangerous and isolated!"*
I knew, but the truth was I didn't and felt I was in too deep to turn around.

I did one more trip, finished loading Frosty and then, came the moment of truth. Would my faithful steed start? She was covered with a thick layer of ice and snow, and looked like she has been put into a cryogenic sleep. I turned the ignition on and the headlight turned on. "Good!" I gave a full shot of throttle (Even though it is fuel injection) because I know that it makes the difference between starting and not starting. I hit the starter button and with the sounds only a hibernating bear would make after a long winter sleep, she started. I got back inside while she warmed up and walked to the miners. They asked me all sorts of questions, and after about twenty minutes of laughter and chat, one of them asked me not to pay attention to those who say it cannot be done, because they are only jealous and wished they could do something like this themselves.

A few of them shook my hand as they walked out to their bus that had just arrived. The door opened unto a world of wind, ice and snow that must be experienced to be understood.

One by one they boarded the bus who looked just as cold inside as it was outside. I watched them and it impressed me. These men were men. Not metro sexual wannabe men!

They looked like men, stood like men and acted like men. None of these guys had better nails, hair than my mom, and they dressed like men too.

Hard working-life grabbing-no nonsense men. The way men were intended to be.

I walked out behind the last one, and even though I dressed the part: I did not feel like it. I was out here playing, and they were out here living it.

I walked to Frosty who by then had warmed up a bit. How warm can something get breathing -40C air?

Even the air flow coming out of her exhausts did not feel hot.

I sat on here rock hard seat and took off following the bus. Even though there was a universe of contrast between them and I, I enjoyed the comedy that it was.

A bus load of hard working miners going to one of the hardest environment, and in one- of not-the hardest climates one can be in doing that kind of work followed by a little motorcycle that should be there only in summer.

Maybe the fact the miners inside the bus were all staring at me was giving me confidence, or maybe, just maybe it was the pride in me that was just thawing out; it was a feeling I still remember vividly

When we hit the intersection where the bus turned towards the mine and I toward Labrador City, they waved at me and we both disappeared from each other's sight in a cloud of white powdery snow.

Shortly after, I saw the Trans Labrador Highway sign into Newfoundland approaching.

This was it! I was there. This is Labrador. I am on my bike in -40C temperatures, and these roads as well as the people around here have never seen a bike at this time of the year. In the next few days I will find out why.

This was it

I was there! The TLH was there right in front of me waiting. What a rush it was!

As I got closer, a Sureté du Québec GMC Suburban came towards me, slowed down, turned around and parks right on the other side. The driver's side windows came down as I was getting off the bike and he said *"Hi Paul! We have been expecting you and were looking for you! "We knew you were at The Wall and were keeping an eye on your movement because we wanted to wish you good luck"*.

Two members of the Sureté du Québec were looking out for me. They knew I was coming and that I had slept at the wall. They kindly offered to take a picture of me by

These SQ guys were great and very friendly. They were my first contact as I entered the TLH in Labrador and somehow made the TLH feel warmer that morning.

Thanks guys! You are scholars!

They saw I had my camera and offered me to take a picture of me by the sign. This sign was THE thing I had been looking forward to see. This sign was more than a sign to me. It was the final step toward something that has been testing me beyond my wildest dreams.
THIS was to me the last frontier. My last frontier!
Many consider the TLH as an accomplishment that they know will talk about for years to come.
To me it was that and so much more. It was the end of wondering whether or not I could make it to Goose Bay. It was also the beginning of the last part of this ride; which for many was just impossible. I do not want to sound conceded, but it was also a testimony to my stubbornness, determination and my will to finish what

I started. But let's not get ahead of things here! I still had another 500 kms to Goose bay and then I had to do it all over again. Another 1100 kilometres!
The officers took a couple pictures of me. They were really nice guys. We chatted a bit on the side of the road, they wished me good luck and I went on to Tim's in Labrador city where I would also phone Peter and Heather from the North 53 Magazine for the interview.

I barely had time to sit down with my coffee and breakfast when they showed up.

The North 53 magazine crew

Peter and Heather

We had a great time with the interview as the locals stopping by for their daily injection of Black Plasma also joined on the fun.
They had to look at this guy who had just showed up in their necks of the wood on a bike.
They were drawn in by Frosty parked right by the entrance beside the drive thru. It was great! They had heard about me but didn't believe it. Nor could they understand why on earth someone would do something like this.

They said they have never seen or heard of anyone coming through in winter on a motorcycle. Cool! While were there, Mike Power from CBC radio showed as well and asked me if I would mind stopping by the radio station that is at the same mall than the Tim's and give him the chance to interview me. *"I would love to Mike! But it is YOU that is giving the chance, not me!"*

Mike Power from CBC National Radio

Mike did not only interview me; but also opened his home for me and treated to a diner kings don't even get. Mike? You are not only a gentleman but also a true representation of what Labrador people are.
Thank you!

I finished the interview with Peter and Heather which was a lot of fun. They wanted to know everything about the trip and I told them. They also said that the interview would show up in the North 53 magazine. Sure enough! It made it in the magazine even the next day.

By the time I reached Goose bay, the rest of Labrador knew I was there.

I went to meet Mike. We sat in the studio where he asked me a few things, and then asked me if I would mind going outside with him so he could make an interview with a sound track to air on his program that day. "Sure!" But maybe you-will mind Mike! It is pretty damn cold out there!" He looked at me puzzled and said *"Really? You know that, and still you are here on a bike in January!"*

As we did the interview outside people who were inside the mall had to come out because of a fire alarm, and gathered around Mike and I.

They saw Mike who is obviously well known in this part of the land, and if he was out here with a mike in his hand, there had to be a good reason. Most of them are born here and I know they do not fool around with how deadly and cold these parts can be. And here I was on a bike!

We spent about fifteen minutes and said goodbye after I promised I would phone when I would be back to TC and go for dinner at his place.

I also had to do a few things. First-I had to go sign in at the Two Seasons Hotel for when I would come back this way. I also wanted to sign on and get my Satellite phone. Not because I wanted it; but because I had promised Melanie and my friends back home that I would.

The satellite phone that you can get for free in Labrador City. Just return on your way out. Nice touch!!

I also had to fix my windscreen. Let me explain this best I can. Last night on the road around the Fire Lake mine, all the bolts holding my windshield but one fell off. The vibration and the roughness of the road finally got the best of the only bolts I had not put LockTite® on. (Murphy's Law) If I ever meet this Murphy I am going to kick his ass so hard that he will have to loosen up his tie to fart. It was dark, windy, snow was flying everywhere, and I could not find a place to pull over and repair. Last thing I wanted was to become a hood ornament while I was trying to fix this.

But luck was on my side and drove by an emergency phone station ten minutes after my windshield spun clockwise pointing to the six O'clock position. Not impressed! So I pulled over and undid the last bolt holding the windshield.

I am lucky it did not fall off completely and did not go under my wheels. Looking back, I would not have been able to make to Goose Bay without some form of wind protection.(You will see why later)

After farting around and cussing like a logger in the cold freezing my fingers off fiddling around with Tabarnac de colisse de petite bolts la. Could they make them smaller for F&^%#$ sake? Sincreme de sacrament de souffleux de trombone de frère bande de crisses de soeur blindee de ciboire my fingers were hurting and I kept dropping the littlest little rubber washer about 100 tabarnac de fois in the colisse de snow. St- ciboire it was time I finished otherwise calver I would have garocher le crisse de windshield in the face of the next one who asked me if I was crazy to ride in this. Souffleux de trombone de mule ensoleillée de crisse! Ok! Where was I?

Translation! You do not want to know! But let's just say it has something to do with me freezing my fingers off fiddling with the most stupidly small bolt and kept dropping the damn socket in the snow, which in turn allowed me to perfect my swearing in French. At this point if someone had stopped and asked me if I was ok, I would have stuffed the windshield up their ass.

Souffleux de trombone de mule ensoleillée de crisse!
Ok where was I? Back to the Two Seasons Hotel

After I picked up the satellite phone at the hotel, I started looking for a place where I could find some metric bolts to replace the ones I have lost.

I made it to the local Ski-Doo® dealer where I found the bolts. It was great except the guys in there all looked like the most miserable pieces of sorry crap I had ever seen. And believe me! I have seen some miserable people while I was working for the government! Topic change! I always said that if you do not like your damn job, just quit and go somewhere else. Anyways! After being told I had to pay about $5.00 for four little stinking bolts, I wanted to tell them to F%$$@ off, but I was in Labrador City and metric bolts are as popular around here as your mother crashing on your prom night! Pissing off the only people who had my bolts in stock was not an option. I paid the man and took off. It was almost 11:00 and Churchill Falls still seemed so far away. My original (Original being the key word) was to stop for the night in Churchill Falls. I left Labrador city at 11:45 Am. DAMN! I had another 560 kms to Goose bay! I was starting to entertain the idea of riding at night. Again!

I left LC and the wind picked up like hell and the thermometer went Deep South. It was still great though. They say the road from LC to Churchill Falls is smoother and wider but that the shit hits the fan past Churchill Falls! We will see!!!

Within 50 clicks winter met with me. I thought it was already there with me. I was wrong. It was not quite there, and it sure let me know. Later on going toward Churchill Falls, I came across a pickup truck, and the driver waved at me to stop. The guys in the pickup truck had to stop me to check me out. I turned around and park in front of them.

The driver poked his head out of the window and asked me if I was ok (Redundant question) and what the hell I was doing there. These guys were born and raised here and they were just coming back from a snowmobile trip that they had to cut short because it was too cold and too much snow to reach their cabin!

These sledders had some great advice for me. Thanks guys!

I was thinking *"Hmmm! And I am here on a bike!?"* A couple minutes later a rig rolled by and saw a bike in front of a pickup truck. The trucker slowed down and stopped besides us and asked if we are ok with a puzzled look on his face. I told him that all was good. He gave me the thumb up and took off.
The guys in the pickup were still freaking out about me. They just couldn't believe this. They asked if they could take a picture because their buddies would not believe them.
We chatted and laughed a lot for about twenty minutes and they warned me about many fresh caribou tracks. I did not take their advice lightly because I knew this was their stomping grounds, and if they were worried; I should be too.
I took off and I could not get my eyes off the spectacle that was opening in front of my eyes.
The scenery was changing right in front of my eyes. The more I drove north, the more the more obvious the isolation and desolation became. I was reminded in a beautiful way that I was in THE MIDDLE OF NOWHERE!!!

Beautiful and yet so unforgiving

Where else can you ride for so long and see nothing at all? It was sobering! This was something I had not felt before! Or maybe I had; but never to this point. The isolation and unforgiving beauty were so in my face.

I knew I was alone last year, when they closed the TCH on me, but I also knew there always were some people nearby. Not here!

Not a soul! Something happens to you here, you can kiss your sorry frozen ass good bye!

I arrived in Churchill Falls at around 4:00 PM. I stopped at the Irving gas station and asked the people there where I could eat and possibly stay for the night. They pointed me to the Churchill Falls Hotel, the only place in town. The guy at the pump was saying that he normally doesn't even get out of the store to fuel trucks and sleds, but that this; he had to do.

After the usual "Are you nuts" the wished me the best and I followed the scent of food and warmth.

When I got to the hotel, a lady who works at the grocery store came running out just as I was about to walk in. Someone at the gas station had phoned her and told her I was on my way. She looked at me and said *"You know- everyone thinks you are crazy!"* And as she said that a guy coming out of his truck said *"This is our way to tell you that we are envious! You chose to do it when so many wouldn't!" Good luck man!"* This was a nice thing to hear after the day I just had.

After ten gallons of coffee and a small Pizza I left for Goose Bay. It was about 6:00 PM. It was dark, it was colder than when I got here; and it was starting to snow. It was dark out when I got there, but it was beyond dark now. The half clear sky had been replaced by one filled with snow. It was snowing quite bit and I was wondering if what I was about to do was really worth doing.

I knew there were plenty of rooms available at the hotel and that I should get one and make it to GB tomorrow. But something inside me told me I should attempt to ride the 300 kms tonight.

Looking at this sign still brings wild feelings in my mind as to how daring and unsafe riding at night in Labrador was. Still 285 kms to Goose bay!

I weighted in all the pros and cons and after seeing that I couldn't scare myself enough to stay put I took off. It was freaking dark! Many places are dark once the sun goes down, but most of the time there is this backlight coming from the surrounding towns lighting up the darkness a bit. None of this here! When it gets dark here! It is 100% dark. After I took a picture of the sign announcing that there are 285 kms of dark isolated, rough beyond belief road ahead of me, I turned Frosty off to feel the night. I could not see ten feet ahead of me.

Better have a flashlight when you break down here because you could not even see your bike or engine. It was beautiful and peaceful in its own scary way. I felt alone! Very alone! I also felt small, non important. Like a little speck on the Labrador scenery that could be wiped out and disappear without anyone ever knowing. Let's recap here! Goose Bay was 285 kms away, it was shit pit dark, they were forecasting fifteen centimetres of snow and judging by how hard it was falling-they were right. The winds were strong, the temperature was around minus 30°C without the wind chill factor and I did not know the road.

Did I mention the caribous were migrating? There were more caribous migrating to this area then men to newspapers stands when the Sports Illustrated Swimsuit Edition comes out.. And oh yes! I was on a motorcycle, alone in one of Canada's most remote, if not the most remote area and just to add to the fun; 2200 kilometres of ice road. So why was I here again??? Just because I wanted to!

That night I am sure if you had opened up my skull/brain, all you would have heard would have been the deafening sound of an empty vacuum-like void. I was on a mission, determined to make it to GB

Anyway! About an hour after Churchill falls (40 KMS) I stopped to rethink all this. The road was so rough and my bike had to be suffering somehow. (I will have a lot of bolts to re-torque) And for the third time in two days I was contemplating the idea of calling it quit. There was risk-and there was this! But I did not! It was just a thought. After about ten minutes I took off thinking, *"Paul! You made it this far! He will take you there! Just do not do anything stupid and take your time! You get to GB when you get to GB!"*

Forty five minutes later my I was feeling the consequences of my first mistake of the day. You know that pizza?? Well-it wanted to go play in the snow! Yep! The wind was blowing, the mercury was way down the scale, you could freeze the balls of a brass monkey and I had to stop like------------------------------ NOW???

Yep! What was my mistake? Taking my coat and gloves off! Dropping my pants in the freezing, snowing wind and answering the big # 2 call of nature! I tried to hold it. Really! I really did. But I could not wait for the next sign announcing the next bathroom because they are rare up there. I climbed off Frosty, to her relief I am sure, and like I said; stripped.

By the time I was done leaving something for the caribou, and finished sliding up and down the snow bank bare ass!, F%$#@ the bidet! My fingers, ass, nuts and all other exposed parts of my lower body were frozen.

I suited up hoping that I would dry and thaw out quickly. But after a couple of minutes I knew I wouldn't. My body was hurting, and my fingers were starting to go numb. I was having some déjà-vu.

I stopped and Rene's tarp came in handy AGAIN! Why didn't I think of this while I was parked on the side leaving something on the side of the road that would embarrass Boo Boo-is still a question I ask myself.

I got off the bike, opened the hack, put the heater together, lit it up, and wrapped myself in the tarp. As I was standing there with the heater at my feet inside my cocoon, I am sure I looked like a large beige Christmas tree or some kind of weird Tee-pee.

The heat from the heater stayed under and I warmed up in about ten minutes!

I put my shit back in the hack (Not that one) and got back on the road. Thanking the hack and Rene again for saving my hide once more.

About ten kilometres past the halfway mark I came across my first caribou herd. I was coming down at about 60 km/h-when Boom! Here they were-right in front of me. It was windy, snowy, and slippery and I was on a hack! YOU DO THE MATH!!! Not the best setup to stop in a hurry.

Remember the snow bank ride outside of Manic 2? Well this looked like I was about to do an encore I slowed down by about two inches an hour, and managed to swing around most of them except one, which managed to hit my left panniers! 'Shit man! That was close! I stopped and gave my ass enough time to let go of the seat. About 75 clicks from Goose Bay I came across my second Caribou herd. But this time I was more prepared! I had noticed a lot of tracks on the road and on the side of the road for the last hour and a half. This meant there were fuzz balls not too far ahead. Big freaking fuzz balls with antlers that could hang me like underwear on a clothe line.

This time I was going slower and I approached them slowly enough that they had enough time to see me and start galloping away from me. There were probably 50 of these magnificent creatures. At least; the ones I could see.

The night slowly went by and I rode slowly. 40- 60 km/h was about all I could do. I had come close enough to disaster that night that pushing my luck any harder was not something I wanted to do.
Another 45 minutes went by and this time I hit the mother lode. I do not know how many there were; but there were a lot of them.
They showed up in a curve and even though I am sure they heard me coming, they were in no hurry.
Maybe they somehow communicate together, and the first herd that came upon the mess I left on the snow bank told these to let me know they were not impressed.

There were a lot, they were all big and they were all just standing there. I slowed down and I ended up in the middle of the pack. For a second or two they stared nervously and started running. Don't ask me why but I started moving with them. Imagine if you can the spectacle that this was. All I could see were legs and shadows dancing on the road. I was surrounded and I could feel the sound of their hooves pounding on the hard ice. They picked up speed, and as they did so did I. But they kept running. They all moved towards the shoulder one at the time as if they were herding me.

As I passed them they looked at me with their head turned towards me and I could see the light shining on their eyes.

They did not all move over though. At one point there were about 6-7 of them running with me and they would not get off the road! They were just running to where I was going. I tried to grab my camera in my tank bag but the wind reminded me very quickly it was not a good idea to let go of the handlebar like this!

Let's just say that whoever would have found me in the spring would have known what my last actions were. The last shot on my camera would have been of a caribou's ass in focus and in the background a huge snow bank approaching. "Yep! I knew Paul! He died snapping a picture of a caribou's ass!" one of my friends would have said in the eulogy.

Anyway eventually they headed for the ditch one at the time, except for the big one in front of the pack. He must have been the leader because he was the biggest and he just looked like it. As he ran in front of me he looked to the left and as he did his left hoof hit my auxiliary light on my hack knocking it backward shining at me. Then he looked to the right and headed to the right shoulder. And as he did, his right hoof hit my jerry can off its rack, tearing it right off and breaking the bungee straps sending it sliding down the road.
I stopped and he kept running for another 50 feet, and then he stopped right on top of the snow bank looking at me.
I got off the bike and picked up my jerry can off the road, turned my light back forward and he took off. I got another bungee strap, tied the jerry can back down and took off again. It was quite an experience. Talk about close encounter of the furry kind! This big bull must have been 1500 lbs! Looking at him run in front of me like this with his head up, the top of his antlers must have been-I dunno-13 feet high?
I was not scared or tensed. I was just in awe. The glass is either full or half empty.
How many have had the chance to witness such beauty in such an environment?

Not too long after that I was just going down the road and I noticed that when I was hitting on the gas the wheel would spin.

The fresh snow on top of the ice road made it feel like a skating rink. I did not have that much traction anymore as I was starting to float on the snow. I started going down a hill, a long hill and I as I reached the bottom I saw very quickly that I had to climb back up faster than I came down if I wanted to make it back up..
I gunned it a bit and Frosty reacted by spinning her back wheel easily as to tell me *"Don't F%$#@ around! We have to make it up!"*
I shifted in 4th gear and started climbing. I did not want to give it gas, and I knew I could not lose more traction because I would not make it up the hill.

Then the sound of the wheel starting to spin, with the speedometer needle slowly going back told me that if I were to make it up I had to just let Frosty do what she wanted. So I let her! About two minutes later I reached the top of the hill in fourth gear at about 4500 RPM and my speed was maybe, 10 km/h. To this day I am still sure I saw this big caribou bull slowly walk besides me as I struggled my way up the hill and said *"Hey Shithead! How you doin?"* I was that slow!

Forty five minutes later I entered GB. I stopped at the Irving gas station to fuel where a bunch of kids cheered me on! Cool! I also noticed that the rear parking light on the hack was not working.
The reason was that the road (Bad freaking bumpy, potholey like hell road) shook off the bolt holding my hack fender on the frame and it rubbed in the tire. No harm done to the fender, but it grooved my tire and broke the wire off the light socket! I would fix that tomorrow morning! I just took a large Zip tie off the tool kit and zip tied the fender enough to make it to the Hotel North.

The fender rubbing on my hack tire had done quite a groove. Luckily enough it was on the side rubber blocks and did not affect how the tire handled

Half an hour later I was at the North hotel. It should be called the **"Bet your ass it is north"** hotel. Frosty was fine and had 7546 more kilometres on her clock.

They were forecasting 60 km/h winds the next day with accumulations of five to ten centimetres of snow and temperatures of -38 in the afternoon without the wind chill. I wanted to leave the following day, but I was hurting, I was exhausted and was getting more tired by the minute. The adrenalin was being pumped in less and less now that I had made it. The toll it had taken on my body and mind was starting to show; and I knew I would be hurting a lot more shortly. I was feeling the same way I did when I reached Cape Spear Newfound-land in 2007. Sitting there quietly on Frosty, thinking silently about what I had just done, completely done for and giggling in my helmet it was very freaking obvious I had to rethink my plan to leave the following day.

As a matter of fact, I had to rethink the idea of crossing Canada again period! I had tears in my eyes that just wouldn't stop. I was so burnt out! But I was also so happy I had made it. It was at that moment that all the chances I taken on my way down here showed up in my mind in a series of ongoing images that would just not stop. Hundreds of them, just ganging up on my mind. This was THE most incredible adventure I had ever been on.

I know! I know! There are no words and there is no way I can explain how I felt at that very moment. One thing struck me more than the others though. I was alone in GB and no one was there to cheer me or take care of me. This was something I started alone and finished alone. I don't want to imply that Harry was not part of this. I am referring to what was to me my biggest challenge. The TLH! I had done it, and I had done it alone!
I attacked it alone; I went through it alone and was alone when it allowed me to win. I would like to think that this is how many adventures end. No fanfare, no celebration, nothing. Just time to sit and think about what just took place. As I paced around the parking lot looking around, I tried to backtrack and see the whole road in one image but I could not! When I cross Canada every year I always visualize the road I have travelled on when I get back home and see it as one line on a huge map in my mind. But today in Goose Bay I could not!

I reached in my tank bag and looked at the map of Canada. I had not looked at it for a while! It was dark, but the Hotel's parking lot light was shining on the map. My eyes did a quick scan from the left of the map to the right and stopped on Goose Bay which I had highlighted with a marker. I was looking at a 24 inch long black line with the word "Start" on one end and "Finish" with a question mark at the other. It was done!

Boom! It hit me again! It forced me to take a deep breath. Right there and then, the realisation of what I had just done sunk in a bit deeper. All of it! I was shaking and I was crying uncontrollably. It felt good! It was like I had wrapped my gut in a steel belt to hold my breath for close to 8000 kilometres and now I could release it. I had trouble breathing.
It was a good thing I was alone. Raw emotions like these are best experienced alone. It is too overwhelming and debilitating to share.

I remembered how I felt the year before when I reached Cape Spear. It was powerful because it was my first

Cross Canada trip in winter. This alone made it something that cannot be duplicated. But the TLH trip was something else.

As I paced around I could feel the strength (Whatever I had left) evaporating out of me. I was getting weaker and weaker by the second, and I could not stop laughing as I cried. Good drugs! *"Chu got it Man! Wantchew pass me some more o that shit man!?"*

Alone, with no one around I fell on my knees... Crying uncontrollably I could feel the tears freezing on my baklava and on my face. Holding my head in my hands I leaned on my elbows on Frosty and felt like I was somewhere else.

Few mumbled words came out of my mouth. I could not strop trembling and I couldn't stop crying. No one knew I was here yet. THIS-WAS-ALL-MINE!

After a few minutes of this, I got back on my feet and tried to wipe my eyes and face, but whatever was flowing out of my eyes and nose was now solid ice.

I took my helmet off and peeled the baklava off my face.

It was now very obvious that the last two days and 1146 kilometres had gotten the best out of me. The scariest ride I had ever been on was now HALF over with.

Tomorrow I would be staying here. Leaving was not an option anymore. I would have to wait another day. The thought of going back was making me shake my head. I walked toward the hotel door laughing and talking out loud. It must have been quite a thing to look at. Thinking about the ride from Baie-Comeau to here I thought that maybe it was not the pizza but that maybe, just maybe, I had finally done something that scared the living shit out of me.

I walked at the front counter of the North Hotel and the lady looked at me like-well-you know!! We chatted a bit and she told me that she had heard I was coming from Amy who was coming to see me tomorrow to give me an interview for the local paper tomorrow. "Shit! I had forgotten about this!" I signed up, went to my room to drop some stuff and walked back outside to park Frosty by the window of my room.

Some habits are hard to kill! After I unpacked my stuff and settled in, I walked outside and stood by Frosty for a bit. The wind was howling between the hotel and the restaurant next door. Snow was swirling around and I knew that when I would wake up in the morning Frosty would be buried in snow. I just stood there and looked at her quietly idling; and the thought of turning her off for a few days did not sit well with me.

She had become so much more than a motorcycle to me. What I saw in her was I am sure, the same thing a dogsledder sees when he looks at his dogs. He sees life! He sees his life through the eyes of his dogs. He sees beyond the animal/human equation. He sees creatures who each have a name, and that he can talk to.

He sees creatures he knows he can count on with absolute certainty. He knows that at any moment during the trek, his life would hang on a thread, if for any reason they were to let him down. But he knows they would never do this, and that they will give him all they have and then some. There is an accord between them, a bond, that is unspoken, and yet as solid as rock.

I felt this looking at Frosty. I saw my steed! I could see her little engine cooling down. I could see her finally rest. And I believe that she knew we had made it and that the credit was hers. I looked at her lines, nooks and crevices a thousand times during this trip, and I knew that I could read her and feel her; and that somehow she could feel me too. If you are not a motorcyclist, this might be hard to understand and even harder to believe. But nevertheless it is the truth. I told her "Merci Frosty!!" Thanks sweetheart! I touched her shield and bars and I was connected to her. *"Goddammit I still have tears in my eyes as I write this"* and *NO I don't need freaking counselling!* At that point I wanted to take her in the room so she could warm up. But I knew that it would harm her more than anything else. I am sure the dogsledder feels the same way at the end of the day when he sees his furry friends laying down outside in

the snow after a long day or week fighting the cold and the elements. They are at ease and resting, laying there on the ground with their fur covered with snow and a little puff of smoke coming out of their mouths as they fall asleep outside. This is also where Frosty is supposed to be. I turned her off; I wished her Good night and walked in. THIS was her day, not mine. This was HER victory, not mine. It is not I who took her here, but her who took me here. To Goose Bay Labrador, the most north eastern point in Canada! And if you do not believe this, well; it is your freaking problem not mine!
I went back in, lied down and fell asleep.

Good night!

Day 18

January 19, 2008
Arrived in Goose Bay Labrador
-38 C at 29453 kms

Here she is in Goose bay Labrador. With almost 8500 kms more on her than when we left home. She made it and in the process took me with her. That morning the temperature was -40C. It had snowed quite bit that night and she was stuck in the snow and almost completely covered. I swept her, moved her in a clear area of the parking lot to do a bit of maintenance on her.

Judging by how I felt when I got up I knew I had made the right choice by spending one more day in Goose Bay. Plus the weather had turned like they said it would. It was already -40C and getting colder. My nemesis (The Weather Channel) was saying that it was supposed to get a lot worse before it got better. They were forecasting lows in the -60C which according to them would be a fifty year record low. My luck! This trip was not supposed to end here, so why would the weather loosen its grip on me now? Last I checked spring came around April here!

Frosty needed some TLC. I needed to adjust her chain, fix the fender on the hack and check her thoroughly. When I went outside the parking lot has been cleared. I brushed the snow off her and moved her to a place where I could lay down and do what I had to do.

Working on Frosty and Goose Bay

Frosty had survived pretty well so far. Nothing had broken off, except for that bolt on the hack fender. I checked everything from the wires to the chain and the sidecar mounts. Everything was still there except the screws holding the sidecar rear light lens. You would think that something built to ride on Russia's roads would have stronger bolts and screws! Well! I guess not! Other than that, the hack had done as well as Frosty. The TLH had been brutally rough, and the fact that she was still running well was a testament of how great a bike she is.

I would have to go to a hardware store to get some bolts and screws. As I was lying down in the snow a fellow came to me and asked me what I was doing here in

winter. As he listened to me I am sure he just thought "Hmm! I wonder if I should call the asylum and let them know I found their last escapee!"
Turns out he's a motorcyclist himself and quite an adventurer too. He is a helicopter pilot and he had work to do for a forest company or power company around here. We chatted for a while and we found out we lived not too far from each other. He gave me a hand by handling mw the tools as I adjusted the chain on Frosty. The wind was brutal and the snow was flying everywhere at times. At one point the wind blew the tool kit off my seat and all my tools ended up on the ground in the snow. Dammit! I will have to bring them in, dry them up because they would rust in no time sealed inside the pouch.

We shot shit some more and exchanged info on each other. I finished my work and went back in. I had not put all my layers on and I could feel the cold outside. Besides the odd snowmobile going by, there was not much life happening around here.

I grabbed a shower and cleaned myself up a bit. Amy from the Goose Bay newspaper was coming soon and I did not want to look and smell like a modern day Daniel Boone. No offense to any outdoorsman here!
She showed up when she said she would! Who told her I like punctuality? She is very young. I was expecting someone older then her doing this kind of job so far up north east. She got her education as a journalist and went where she wanted to work. In her home town! We spent about an hour chatting and laughing. She said this was big news in GB. Action like this does not happen often around these parts. She said they see a few bikes in summer but not many. Sleds are the vehicle of choice around here in January, not motorcycles!
After the interview she asked me if I would mind going outside and ride my bike up and down the street so she could take pictures of me. "Of course I don't mind Amy" I told her I would go out and start Frosty and that we

would have to wait about 20 minutes for Frosty to warm up.

We went outside and I made a couple passes by her on Frosty as she snapped shots. Once we are done she told me that she had to go to the A&W to meet her boyfriend on his snowmobile. She did not have a car and her grandma had given her a ride to the hotel.

I sat her in the sidecar and drove her to the A&W where everyone in there had showed up riding a snowmobile. They looked at me and gave me the thumbs up. I let Amy out, told her thanks for taking the time for me and we parted. This young lady will go far.

Then I went to the hardware store where I hoped I could find a couple of long weird screws that would fit a Russian sidecar. I was sure I had better chances of finding a politician looking for the truth in a fishing lodge. But guess what? I found them.

The folks at the counter let me test a few and lent me the tools to do it. (My tools were in the room drying) After fiddling around for a few minutes outside my fingers were like Popsicles and they were hurting like Maudit Colisse!

Frosty was running, so I just took my gloves off a bit and stuck them one at the time at the end of the muffler so the hot exhaust gases warmed them up, and slipped them back on over my frozen fingers. It worked well! This would become routine during this trip. About half an hour later I was done. A few locals stopped by and took pictures of me as I was working on the bike. $3.00 later I was heading back to my room.

The feeling I had when riding in Goose Bay's frozen roads that day was something that must be experienced. Realizing that the road I was on ended right there in front of me. This was it! You could go no further. One block from my room was the END. The road was lit by the sun barely floating above the horizon and listening to the snow squeaking under my wheels at minus forty

This is the end of the road in Goose Bay! The sun setting in the west and the snow blowing across the ice covered road was showing me this was as far north I could go on this side of the country. It was -41C when I took this picture. And believe me, it felt like it!

something I knew this was it. This was what I had come here for. It was absolutely amazing.

This shot to me is Pure Goose Bay! Without words it shows the nature and beauty of the place but also the lack of forgiveness this place would show me if I were to play with her senselessly and carelessly. I was a guest in her midst, and nothing reminded me of this more than the biting wind and cold I felt in the air today.

It was as if she was telling me *"You are welcome here my friend! Play by my rules and do things my way, and I might let you out. Laugh at me, or underestimate me, and I will hurt you in ways you never thought were possible!"*
I thought that my trip last year had showed me how powerful Mother Nature can be. Now, a year later in Goose Bay Labrador I knew she was a good teacher! I remembered my lesson! Labrador has showed me more

than this. It had showed me that so far, luck had been a big player in this adventure, and that my understanding of myself and how far I knew I could push my limits was not the main reason why I had made it. I did not know yet exactly what the whole lesson would teach me, but I knew the lesson was not over. I still had to pay attention. She is not the type of teacher that will smack you on the head or just toss an eraser at you. The lesson she gives are unforgiving. The game I was playing could be played only one way. Pay attention! Or go home in a box!

Feeling this intensely, knowing that I was just a speck of dust that had landed on her, and that I could be dealt with as such, was not only a very sobering thought; it was also in some kind of way; comforting. It was clear and it was finite. No doubts at all! It also reconfirmed that even though sometimes I felt otherwise, that I was not after all doing this blindly, and that my pride about my accomplishment so far was no reason for celebration. I still had to do the same thing. AGAIN!

This was what really scared the hell out of me! It really did! I knew now that it would be colder! It would also feel longer because I now had expectations based on experience. I would have the opportunity to think things like "I *have seen this!*" or "T*his thing is coming"* etc and *etc. A*nd this way of thinking can only allow one thing to happen. Fuck ups! From now on, my mind could play games and become lazy.

Not really the appropriate tape to play over and over in my mind. Where was I? Oh yes! I went back to my room where I would spend the rest of the day resting and writing my notes, as well as making some phone calls.

By now everyone knew I had made it here. Everyone knew I had accomplished what I set out to do; and that I could turn around right now and quit. No one could fault me for it. But I had made up my mind and had decided to ride back to Victoria. The determination I had when I left was still there, but the energy was not. It was overshadowed by a sense of accomplishment that built some kind of mental laziness in me. It was as if I caught myself saying *"Oh! Whatever! It will be cool!"* It was not cool. I was tired, and I was already fighting with negative thoughts and fear joined in very shortly after. As I turned on the TV and watched The Weather Channel; the news was not good. The -50's and 60's they had forecasted were already in Labrador City. Which meant??? Holy Crap Batman!!

I had never ridden in -61°C temperatures before. I did minus forty something and that was enough. But -61°C? How would I function? How would Frosty function? That was assuming she could function at all. Should I even consider riding in this? *"Holy shit"* was my first thought. My second one was "Holy Shit!" And Holy Shit was all I could think for a while..

Would my gear stand it? The labels say it could, but did I really want to trust my life to labels? There was no doubt anymore that if I made one mistake, I was done for. I gave my SAR buddy a call. Remember I contacted him before I left and asked him what his thoughts were about this idea of mine? This is his playground and he knows what the weather can do to people here.

He picked up the phone and I asked for him, then I heard *"Tabarnac man! Es-tu fou? Osti ca fait 2 semaines que je te suis! T'aurais pu m'appeler hier Tabarnac?* In English *"Holy shit man! Are you fucking nuts? I have been following you for 2 weeks now! Why the hell didn't you call me yesterday?"* I asked him what he thought about me being on the move in the next two days, and what were the chances of me being rescued if something happened.

His answer was short and sweet. *"F%$#@ Man! NONE!!"*
They have grounded the choppers and unless there is some wild change in the weather you are on your own"
Good! At least now I knew not to push the 911 Button! Wouldn't make a damn difference!

We chatted for a bit, and as we talked the friend he is came in and the SAR tech took a hike. He knows how stubborn I am. We were in the forces together and we go back to high school together. As you already know, he knows better than to tell me not to do this.

He wished me luck and promised me that he would be following me and would send reports of my progress and location to others as I moved out of Labrador to maximize my chances. .
"If they can they will be ready to pick you up Paul. Either you or the big pile of dead frozen stubborn shit you could end up becoming! Love you Man!." And he hung up.

The more I watched TV, the more I was freaking out. So I turned the F%$$@ thing off. By now people all over were watching these forecasts and I was getting Emails asking me to get out of Dodge without Frosty, fly back home and come back in the spring to pick her up. To use one of my close friend's Quote: *"Paul this was adventure and it was cool! But now this is just downright stupid and dangerous!"* End Quote.
I was hearing what they were saying and kind of agreed, but I also had this little but very clear voice inside telling me that quitting was not an option. I could do this if I wanted to. After all deep inside of me I still believed I could All I had to do was to stay sharp, conquer my fears as I always do, keep my Teflon underwear on because I would/ could/ might shit my pants as I slip-slide all over this granite hard ice road. Also, second to most important; I had to make sure I left this big horseshoe up my ass. And MOST importantly ask God to help me through it.
By now I was posting my thoughts (Not all of them) on the Blog. I realized that if I wrote down what really took place on this road coming up here, that people close to me could have me committed. This could also cost me relationships with people who love me as they would wonder what kind of person puts love ones through something like this?
All this was going through my mind and my sometimes easy to distract brain cells were working over time. I spent the rest of the evening writing two sets of notes. One that I would post, (The filtered ones), and one that I would keep to myself as they were raw, rough and cut right through my heart.

> **Notes: I did not know at the time, but the things that would happen in the following days would redefine me not only as a rider; but as a man. Limits would be pushed beyond anything I had ever even dreamed.**

I knew I was going to push my body to its extreme limits and putting my brain through sensations and feelings unknown to me so far; but somehow, I also knew it was going to get a lot worse.
I showed the laughing, rough and tough Paul on the blog, but the serious-holy shit-this is tougher than I thought-Paul was not on the blog often. At least not yet! Hey! We all have our own battles!
I had decided that my thoughts were hard enough to deal with, without taking those of others onboard. The afternoon came and went ad before I knew it, it was dinner time.

I had not eaten all day. I put my coat on and walked next door to the restaurant. I walked in and sat down. The waitress came to me and said *"We were hoping you would come over! We had to see firsthand what kind of man does something like you just did! You know people around here play in winter but would never take the risks you took"* I said *"Sometimes I want to say that it felt like a good idea at the time! But at the end of day I am too tired to talk and I shut up"* I was too tired to go on about as to what I do and who I am and what pushes me to do this. I didn't really have the answers to these questions anyway!
I sat over a good dinner and a few cups of hot coffee and worked on some more of my notes.

> ***What follows was what I wrote that day.***
> ***I know some of you might be offended by this and look at me in a different way after you read this. I could apologize for it but I will not. This book is not about being politically correct nor is it about some adventure being romanticized. This is I writing about what I did, and about how I felt.***

These were the notes I wrote while I was in the restaurant.

Tabarnac am I ever F%%$#@ tired? What the hell was this all about? Why? Really! Why? I slept last night like I had been run over by a F%$#@ steamroller and my mind was going 100 MPH. Paul for F%$#@ sake smarten up here? Think? You WILL make it through. Don't get run down and then stay down. Go down! Do your whining! And then get up.

Roll call!
You still love riding? Yes!
You are still happy you can do this? Yes!
You still are healthy and you are still breathing? Yes!
You still have the chance to try and back out? NO!
You want to park Frosty and go home in a plane? No!
You want to at least try to make it out of here? Yes!
Well then-good enough!

Dad? You are laughing up there! I can feel it! I know you and I am sure that right now you are nudging God with your elbow telling Him "That is my boy! Whoops! You know what I mean right!"

I am sure that Ian is right there too and you are telling him some funny things too.

Really dad! What is this all about? I know you have instilled in me strong beliefs about how short life is and how we should all embrace it.

But I have to ask you this. Am I a wimp by going down in flame after something like this and then come back up and move on? Am I losing my mind? Or is it just the way I am made? Tell me!

Last year I felt like a nut case. I felt even though it was just for a few seconds, like a wimp. How could I put myself through this and then go down in flames like this? I flew home last year and felt like I failure. I know I said many things and acted some ways, but is it really necessary for me to collapse before I get back on my feet? Do you remember when Ian had his accident? I saw him hit the ground and I knew he was on his way home to Him. I crawled by his side and just had enough time to hold his hand and tell him how much I loved him and he was gone. The next few hours I watched his cold body laying there under a tarp as we waited for the coroner. I could not breathe, I could not stand and yet I was functioning. How could this be? Once I left him in the hands of the EMT I had to ride back home for two days with my heart and mind so heavy that I could not control my own breathing. And yet I rode home for two days without even coming close to lose control.

I have been tested in ways in my life I cannot even write about. Things I have done that only you know now because you are beside Him. Things that defy logic, law and human thinking! But still! Here I am ticking and rolling and sometimes pissing people off! Ok! Often!

Many questions and so few answers Dad!

It is as if I do enjoy going though this. As a matter of fact I do enjoy it! I love the risk, I love the danger and I love to push the envelope.

Too much some say, and I think that THIS is what my problem is. Somehow I let the others' thoughts and fear get to me and drag me down.

You know last year when I came back home and found myself? Well am I here because I am looking for something, and I do not what it is. Or is it because I need to do this to enjoy who I really am! I know that we ALL like to pose! It is called pride! But this is not why I do this. There is this voice in me I have since I was a boy and I just follow it. So far so good! But shit! Sometimes it is more than I can handle.

I just know that I will get the answer to this question from The Big Guy when it is my time to go home.

Till then Dad! Keep an eye on me! (End of notes)

There were no other customers inside. When the waitress came over to give me a refill I asked her why it was so quiet. Her answer was *"People try to stay in when it is this cold!"* "Ohhh! That makes me feel good!" I finished my dinner and back to my room I went. It was early in the evening but I knew I needed all the rest I could get with what was coming in the next few days.

I knew that as restful as the last two days were, that it was not good for me. I had lost the habit of being outside. It is like training. With temperatures hovering around -60' it was not the perfect condition to see whether or not I still had it. I hit the sack early and spent some time talking to the Big Guy up there. He knows me! After all he created me. I am sure that many times, he wonders why I act like not all my dogs are barking. (See Glossary) I can almost see him sitting on his throne looking down at me, stroking his magnificent white beard and say something like *"HMMM! Maybe I should have worked on something else instead!"* Oh Well! Let's see where this will go! What do you think Marcel? (My dad)
Maybe I will phone down below and make sure that Big Red has not reserved a place for Paul already! Hmmmmmmm! Do I smell a wager here? Naaaaahhhhhh!"

Good night

Day 19

January 20, 2008-01-21
Goose bay, Labrador
-38 and with Wind chill it is -48

I am glad I stayed in Goose yesterday. It was 7:00 when I got up. "Paul! Habille-toi? Tu vas prendre ton coup de mort!" M'man y fa chaud et je n'aime pas avoir chaud! » "Paul Get dressed? You will die out there like this! "But Mom! I hate being hot!" Out I would go skiing in my jeans and jeans jacket with my back showing, while Bruno and dad were dressed like Eskimos.
I would take major falls, get up, scrape the snow out of my T-shirt and keep going. This was nuts. My dad was worried but at the same time knew he could not make me do what I did not want to do!
Time has passed but many things haven't changed. (This) was the scene playing out in my head and the words ringing in my ears as I got outside this morning. Last night the weather channel was saying that it would be minus 40°C this morning without the wind chill. Man! They were not kidding! As I walk by the reception the girl tells me" -50 Paul! Better make sure you are zipped up!"
As soon as I got out the wind and cold hit me like a freaking wall. Frosty was sitting there all alone, frozen solid; and I felt bad for her. She had to spend the nights out, and she was the one doing all the work!
I walked to Frosty and asked her to wake up. I swept the snow off her and broke the ice of the seat. I was convinced she could hear me. I caressed her and asked her to come to life again for me one more time as I hit the start button. She turned but would not fire. She hesitated a few times most likely because she had low grade in her (I am sorry Frosty that is all I could find) and it does not light up the way it normally does.
After a few tries she came to life without backfiring or anything. She was purring clunkily and quietly in the cold Labrador morning air and I could feel her wake up just like I was.
I went inside to get my stuff and walked back out to load her up while she warmed up. This morning I will give

her half an hour. It is a ritual I have learned from last year!

I went in, suited up real good and real tight, and walked back to Frosty. I sat on her and I could feel that the rear shock was frozen because it did that awful squeaky noise and it did not compress.. The seat felt like a rock and even the handlebar will not turn easily. (I will find out when I am back in Quebec and that Frosty is getting her tune-up that the steering head bearing was cut in half) I looked down and said a few words to the Big Guy up there and then asked Frosty to give it one more shot.

I put her in gear and she answered with a loud Clunk and we took off. It was easy to see it was freaking cold because when I grabbed the clutch to shift in second gear, she almost came to a stop. The chain felt like a piece of rebar wrapped around my sprockets. I was on my way to Tim' Horton's. This is the most north eastern one in Canada. As I made my way there I could hear the squeaking of the snow under my tires. I made it to Tim's, and as I got off, I took my gloves off to take a picture of frosty in front of Tim's. I chose not to go inside. I did not feel comfortable going in the warmth this shortly after starting the day. I took a picture of her proudly idling in front and took off again.

I got my gloves liners out and put them inside my gloves. But not before I warmed them up on the tip of my mufflers. Coming out of GB the scene was almost unreal. The face of cold was everywhere in an in your face way. Ice, nothing but ice everywhere! As I climbed the first hill coming out of Goose bay I looked at my thermometer on my tank bag and it reads -51°C. This would be the last time it will show something.

I guess two year and two winter trip was all this little battery could take.

Within half an hour I started to worry. The cold was intense and so far I was doing all right except for my feet that I had to keep moving. This was not right. These boots were tested for -100. I also worried about Frosty and what could go wrong. I did not want to be stranded around these parts any more than the Pope wants to be caught in whore house!

It became obvious quickly that I'd have to stop every fifteen minutes or so, to do my cold bacon dance and move my feet. I did not know why my extremities were starting to feel cold.

I knew something was wrong but I did not know what. It was a strange cold I was feeling, and it felt different.

I could not put my finger on it. I had never felt cold like this before.

After doing this a couple of times I knew I was in deep shit in so many ways it was not even funny!

First I had to take a leak! My suit was frozen solid on me, and it was hard to undo the zipper. I couldn't take the chance to break it. So I lift my coat, undid my zip on my pants and bib and "Holy crap! Where is it?" Oh! There it is!", then quickly reversed the process. By now, my fingers were frozen! I put my gloves on but they were too cold and I could not do what I normally do which is to tuck my gloves under my sleeve. I warmed up a bit by holding my gloves on the muffler's tip and eventually slid them on. This felt good but it should not have been happening.

Minus 50 and it sure felt like it

About an hour outside of Goose Bay I stopped to take this shot. My camera died pretty much as soon as I got it out. The battery was not doing well at -51C.
I had to take a glove off to take the shot. Normally it doesn't take long enough for me to freeze. But this time my finger tips were again frozen in seconds. What the?? I examined my suit just in case there was hole I was not aware of or something like this, but nothing was wrong. My chest felt weird, but then again what should "Not weird" feel like? Muffler warmer time again! I shouldn't have had to this so often. I walked around Frosty and everything looked ok with her. The snow sounded like Styrofoam being crunched. It felt alien to be there.
I got back on Frosty and within five minutes I had to stop again! As good as this helmet is, it has one flaw. The mask sits well over your mouth but because some air gets in in an otherwise sealed environment, the difference between the outside air and the one inside my helmet a thin layer of crystals was starting to build up! At least that is what I thought was going on! I had to figure out what the hell was happening to me.

I had to scrape the layer of frost with my gloves every two or three minutes or I could not see anymore. I felt like my head was inside an ice machine. I tried to compensate by riding with my visor cracked open but within thirty seconds my exposed eyeballs were stinging like hell! Not good!

I stopped to take this shot of me. I was starting to struggle a lot more than I was willing to admit. The following hour or so will push me in ways I still do not like to talk about. I looked many times at the 911 button on my Spot tracker and wanted to push it so much. I was starting to feel pain all over. Even the pain was a pain I had never felt before

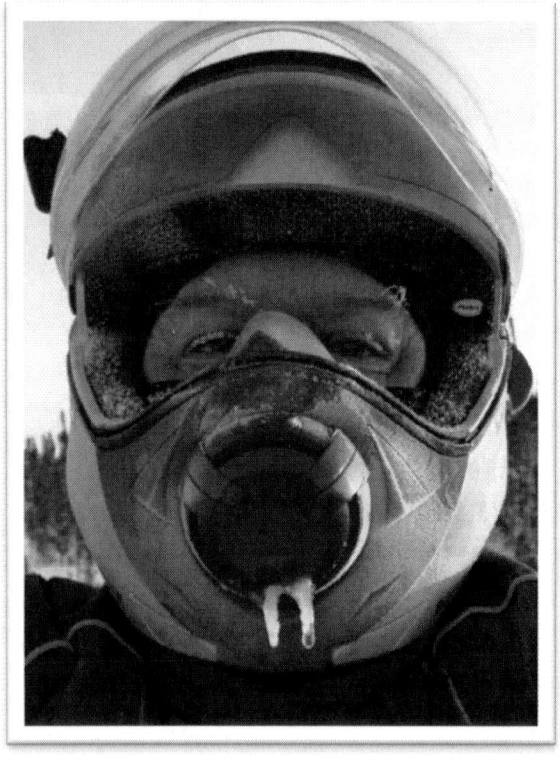

This is the look of Cold

I did not know it at this point but I had made a mistake that could have cost me my life. By the time I took the picture I could only ride for about 10-15 minutes at the time. Somehow I felt as if I was freezing from the inside.

I was fighting something I could not see or touch and I was not winning. My face was getting swollen and it was even getting hard to blink. If you look close you can see my lashes frozen to my eyelids.

Even though I was in serious trouble, the beauty of Labrador was still amazing me. A sky so blue and whites so white it was like living in a perfect post card.
When I stopped to take the following picture my insides were hurting so much I had tears in my eyes. They froze as they went down my cheek and stuck to my baklava like glue.

I could not go on anymore. It felt like my body was solidifying by the second. I was all zipped up. Why? I checked my skin and it was warm and yet I was hurting beyond anything I had felt before.

As I was about to get back on Frosty I saw this puddle of oil under her belly. And it was building up very quickly. I had to fix it and I had to fix it now. This was not the time or the place for her to fail me because she ran out of oil. If I got stuck here I was done; or at least pretty damn close. It had been a couple of hours since I left GB and had not seen a soul.

Pages before: the snow was so white and the sky so blue it was amazing.

Below: this was a site I did not want to see. Frosty was bleeding

Remember my engine case breather return that freezes and sends the back pressure out through a vent problem? Well! I had come up with a solution which is to run an extra line of vent from the engine to under the seat and terminate it with a small K&N filter.

The idea works, but with the mild weather we had in Victoria, I forgot to plug it in before I left. Now what! I could take a picture with my gloves on, but I could not work with small tools. I needed my fingers to unscrew small screws with a small screwdriver or small ratchet, and I had little patience and energy left.

I was literally dancing on the road trying to get the blood going to my digits as I tried to figure what next! I had no choice! I stopped dancing and said "Ok Paul!" Easy does it! I opened up the hack and whipped out my tool kit while Frosty kept running. I did not want to shut her off and I knew that disconnecting the engine case breather hose would be messy even though it would be just for a few seconds.

I grabbed the ratchet and my skin stuck to it. Not the ideal time to fool around with this. I ignored it and kept working. I pulled the 8 mm socket and started to repair.

But I was not getting anything done fast. I was signing and sounded like shit. My throat sounded like I had a cold. I had to fix Frosty. My fingers were starting to bleed as I cut the frozen skin on the clamp holding the hose. I could feel the sensation on my finger tips rapidly vanishing. I walked behind Frosty and heated them up with the muffler while I danced to make sure my feet were ok. Shit! Why was I so cold? I walked back to the right side and crouched back down again between the hack and Frosty and kept working. I eventually disconnected the stock line and I reconnected the custom one. Normally at home this would take about one minute the way I designed it. But in these conditions it took me about half an hour.

By the time I was done I had no feelings left in my fingers. I realized I had gotten in what I call my auto pilot mode. It is as if a switch goes on and all the emotions and feelings go away. I am focused and nothing matters anymore except the task at hand. I know from experience that when I am like this, I am in a place most people would not like to be. The thought of being alone here kept crawling up my mind and I kept kicking it out. I kept saying "What the hell! If it is my time it is my time!

A I write this now I am thinking "You <u>were</u> stranded Paul!" I had been on the road for two hours by now, and had not seen a soul. I couldn't ride more than 5-10 minutes at the time. This was my zone and it was tensed.
I had to go and I had to go now! I repacked my tools and closed the hack. I got back on Frosty smiled at her and asked her if she was ok, then took off. I knew she was! As I rode away the ice in my visor was getting thicker. But I had figured something out already. I kept a piece of towel my tank bag. I'd stop, whip it out and hold it against the muffler tip for a minute. Then I would wipe the inside of my visor.
There is something special about the fresh smell of exhaust in your helmet every ten minutes in the morning that says *"Screw coffee! This beats caffeine as far as waking up is concerned!"* Don't ask me why, but I went past the midway station where I could have stopped and asked the MOT guys for shelter but did not stop. I was thinking many things at that point, and many scenarios were popping in my mind, but hitting the 911 function on my Spot tracker was not yet one of them. I kept working at staying calm. I was trembling and I was wearing what I had always worn so far. One T-shirt, my long sleeve military spec under garment, my fleece liner, and my jacket. Down below I had one pair of sock and my long fleece military spec underwear and my pants. I could add more stuff but I had nowhere to stop to put it on safely. I had ridden what felt like hundreds of kilometres, and yet I was still 130 kilometres away from Churchill Falls. At 70 km/h I would be there in two to three hours at least! I stopped many times, and each time was worse than the last.

Few times I stopped, walked down the road jumping up and down and sat on the snow bank. Not a soul went by. I had still not seen a single vehicle since I had left

Goose bay. I was thinking that if I came across someone; I could wave them down and ask to rest inside their vehicle. Then soon, I started feeling the exhaustion to a point where I could not think clearly anymore. Shortly after that I stopped again and could not go on anymore.

I realized I had only three options. Two of which meant the end of the road for me. 1) With Frosty off I could lie down on the snow bank, tell her Goodbye and wait for the cold to put me to sleep permanently. Or 2) I could push on the 911 function on my SPOT tracker, sit down on Frosty and wait/hope for a Rescue team to come and pry my dead French Canadian maple syrup eating ass off my faithful steed or 3), I could hop back on and die trying to move forward. I choose option number 3.

I rode for what seems a long time. I stopped again and walked a bit. I could hardly walk. I walked back to Frosty and without even hesitating I did what I thought I would never do. I gave up! I looked at Frosty and said *"I am sorry! I cannot go on anymore! I have to shut you down."*

I turned her off and lied down on the snow bank. My options had changed. Pushing the 911 button was absolutely a waste of time for those who would try to come. As I lay there silently and amazingly enough, peacefully and restfully, I heard something.

It was like a crunching sound. Sounded like plastic crackling! "What the F%$#@!"

I sat up and looked around. Nothing! I laid down again looking at the amazingly blue sky and smiled. *"Dammit! It was a good ride! It was good. I have been blessed, and I would do it the same way again! No regrets!"*

All alone, all I could hear was my breathing and that crunching sound! *" Holy shit! What is this?!"*

Except for this sound it was total silence. Beautiful! For a second I thought it was my suit crackling in the cold; but I could see it wasn't.

I was happy when I realized this sound was coming from my lungs. Yes! Happy! I had an answer!

No one around could have heard it. But with my ear plugs and my helmet on I could hear it reverberating in my head. I could also hear my body move. My lungs were frozen! *Shit! That is it! There has got to be something I can do to undo this! What now!* My mind got in second gear!

If you know about surviving in the cold, you know that if you get to a point where your inside are freezing while your outside is still warm, you are suffering (Dying) from what some call "Inverted exposure". I had to think, and I had to think now. *"How the hell is that possible?* Then! Ding" a bell went off. My freaking paper filter! I had not put it in my helmet face mask because I had not brought enough and ran out in GB. In Goose Bay I thought *"Naahh I will be fine!"* but this thought was now biting me in the ass. I tried to take my helmet off and I could not! Everything was frozen together. Mask, baklava, helmet ad my face were one big frozen lump.

Warm air hitting −50°C at 70 km/h will build up ice in a hurry! *"You think?"*

I got up and started Frosty again as I remembered (Duh!) my propane heater. I was obviously not thinking clearly because I should have remembered this way before, and warmed myself up as needed. Amazing what the cold can do, not only to one's body but also to one's brain.

Another Duhness moment! Shit happens!

I started opening the hack but the cover felt like steel. I tried to undo the snaps and all but three broke clean off. I yanked out the propane tank and set up my heater on the ground between Frosty and the snow bank. By now I could not feel anything anymore and it did not matter. I now knew I would be ok.

I reached in my tank bag and pulled out the matches. I opened the box, turned the propane on and I quickly struck one match to light up the heater.

But I had no feelings anymore to any of my extremities and could not hold the match enough and it kept slipping off my fingers.

"Please let me do this ok?" is what I said as I looked up. *"Please?"* After what felt like an eternity, I lit the match

and the heater came to life. Then I put my frozen fingers back in my glove.

I pulled the tarp out of the hack but it was like trying to unroll a sheet of metal. It was frozen solid. But after a few grunts and swears I finally wrapped it around me. Then I squatted over the heater and then heard what I really didn't want to hear. A subtle but yet unfreaking-believably annoying Pop! The heater had gone out.

Maudit St-Colisse de crisse de sacrement de maudit prêtre fifi de calver de sœur blindée d'apocalypse de st-ciboire de Tabarnac de souffleux de trombone de mule ensoleillée d'osti bandage enflée de sin crème! They told me propane freezes or turns into gel at around −38°C. But what do they know? They only live around here for F%$#@' sakes!

I was not a happy camper. *'What now! Think Paul! Think!?*

I pride myself in being tough, but this was testing me beyond anything I have ever done and to be honest, this alone was enough for me as it was.

I thought of something right away! I took the propane tank to the back of frosty, wrapped the tarp around Frosty's rear end and me and held the propane tank near the muffler. The exhaust heart was warming me up slowly and the tank as well.

Squeezed between the bike and I it warmed up in about five minutes. By now the trembling had slowed down. I have been cold in my life and I know a thing or two about it; but this was something else. Having your internal organs freezing while your outside is warm is an experience to be reckoned with. After warming up the tank I walked back to the side of the bike and as I leaned over to pick up the heater, I leaned on the right HypoHandz and hit the kill switch. Silence! Absolute silence! For a second or two I was hearing nothing. Again! I felt warmer and the crunching noise was still there, but not as crisp. By now my lungs were hurting a bit more. But at least I felt them. Good trade in. More pain, easier breathing and less shaking! I stood there warmer up by Frosty looking like a giant frozen burrito.

It took a good half hour. But the warmth was absolutely divine! Never F%$#@ mind! It was orgasmic!

Once I felt I could kind of function again I started repacking things and within minutes was good to go. My shot all packed, sitting on Frosty, I looked up, said thanks and took off. As I took off I asked Frosty to forgive me for even thinking of letting her there all alone.

Note: Today I try to remember if I ever felt so helpless, and I can honestly I never had. I still cannot find the words that explain how I felt. I still have tears as I write this. The exhaustion was paralyzing. I wanted to give up but did not know how. Maybe because I never really give up!

I know many reading this will remember a time when sheer determination combined with despair allowed them to go past what would be considered stupid and survived

I can still feel the terror I felt when I took this last shot of me with my eyes frozen and ice coming out of my helmet where air should be. Don't ask me why with all the shit that was going on I thought of taking a picture. I knew my battery was dead and that it most likely would not even turn on. But it did. I guess standing still; it was warmer in the tank bag? Dunno!

I really could not see how I could make it back to the half way station, let alone keep going to Churchill Falls. The rest of the trip toward Churchill Falls will put me in that same position again, but this time I would do the right thing. I became pretty effective at setting up my heated tee-pee.

The trip meter was showing 155 kms when the reserve light came on! I had been making less than half the 88 MPG I normally average! You think???

Maudit colisse de tabarnac de niaiserie de cochonnerie de colisse! Why don't you give me a F%^$# break for a bit. I was not saying this to Frosty- I was just whining!

I pulled over and untied the two gallons Jerry can on the side of the hack. Then I tried to quickly turn off Frosty so I could use the key to pen the gas cap but it would not turn. It was frozen in the lock!
AAAAAAAAAARRRRRRRRRRRGGGGGGGGGGGGHHH HHHHHHHHH!
Tabarnac the AARRGGHHHHH!
I dropped the can and walked away! "Calm down Paul! You will make stupid mistakes if you keep this up!" It is ok so far! "Kind of-sort of! Whatever!" Think! Think!" My spare key was buried in my luggage! Ding! Ding! An idea came to mind. I took off the tank bag and as I lifted up my jacket and reach for my zipper said *"Forgive me Frosty for peeing on you!"* This would thaw out the lock! Then I remembered the guys at BMW Toronto gave me a little spray bottle of WURTH de-icer.
I reached in the left pannier and there it was. I sprayed it on and Taa-Dahhhh!- out came the key! I was so happy I did not have to pee on Frosty! I refuelled and took off again! About ten minutes later my face was hurting! I had freaking Popsicle growing out of my face! Every time I frown or something I pulled my brows. The shield was still frozen inside and so was my exposed skin. How far to Churchill Falls? Still not a soul in sight! I tried to take more pictures, but the battery was really gone by now. The display showed "Battery exhausted"
Battery exhausted? *What the F%$&# "What do you think my F%$# meter is saying you F%$@!& piece of shit! Let me show you how exhausted you can be? I will shove you up some dead caribou's ass to warm up. Hold on here! Here is an idea! Maybe! Just maybe! If I am lucky enough to find a fresh carcass, slit it open and crawl inside.*
Been done before!   Where was I? Oh yes! The dead battery! I was trying to ignore the pain and focus on something else. This something else was my camera

battery. I was having a conversation with a F%#@ing camera battery.

Here I am, put there trying to have fun and fighting this with all I have, and you give up on me because of the little bit of F%#@ing cold you feel from within the tank bag you ugly stinking piece of tabarnac de shit! $1500.00 for you?

"Calm down Paul! Calm Down! I am sure the animals who were hearing me scream in my helmet were wondering!

I can see it! Two caribou on the side of the road are having the following conversation

-Hey Joe! Isn't that guy normally carrying a gun?
-Yeah!?
-Why is he talking to himself and his camera?
-Don't know! Maybe it is a new gun!
-I don't know, but if it is, I do not think we are his target!
-Yeah! You're right! I think he sounds like he is his own target!
-Well Joe if they are like this guy this season maybe you and I will end having more kids than planned.
-Humma !Humma! what's that I am seeing down there? Bertha!

Maybe there should have been a display on my helmet saying "Life form inside exhausted"

Anyway where was I? Something really cool happened as I was talking/screaming to my camera. I realized that my temperature was going up and I felt warm! HMMMMM!

So for the next 100 something kilometres I was fidgeting on Frosty as I rode and also kept screaming in my helmet. How do you spell Self-inflicted high blood pressure?

With God grace I made it to Churchill Falls where I fuelled up at the same gas station a few days ago. The guys at the counter recognized me and said that they had hoped I would make it back and would stop by again. Here I was again, looking all strong and all that shit, but I was dying inside. After the customary pictures and handshakes I went to the restaurant at the Hotel.

Sitting there in front of a good bucket of coffee, I looked out the window and I could see part of the town buried and asleep under all this snow. I wolfed down a bowl of turkey soup and a large French Fries with Gravy! Hey! I needed to have the freaking protein!

Forty five minutes later when I stopped quivering, I went down and got another pair of socks and a long sleeve sweater. I put my new layers on and went outside. Damn! It had cooled down a few degrees since I had walked in.

Before I could even dream of taking off from there (I know, I know! Why would I even think of it) I had to find a way to get a filter for my mask or make one somehow. As I sipped on my coffee a bright light, well! Not that bright came on in my mind.

Churchill Falls! It had been so cold for the last 2 days that people left their vehicles running all day. The pickup truck owner told me his had been running for 2 solid days.

There is a grocery store downstairs in this complex. I was sure I could find something made of paper that can be used as a filter. As I drank my coffee I thought "Hmmm! *Paper towels? Nope! Butt wipes? Nope! How about something made of cloth? Nope! If these damn filters are made of paper there must be a reason here! Hold on a second here*! as I looked at the coffee grounds in my cup. Coffee filters! Yeah Baby! That is it. *"Thank you coffee grounds"* I ran downstairs and bought a pack of 100 filters. The non bleached ones! I will be breathing through these things and I am already doing enough things that could kill me as it is without breathing this ink poison. I got back outside to Frosty who was idling quietly and grabbed my Leatherman Wave Multi tool. I got back to another cup of coffee (No grounds please!) and started cutting the filters into shape. They were quite a bit thinner than the original ones so I had to stack about five of them to make one mask filter. I put it in and it looked just like the real thing. I was sure it would be better than nothing. I had this weird sensation in my chest and throat as I drank my hot coffee. I was hoping that this freezing would not cause permanent damage to me throat, airways and lungs.
If these filters didn't work I would really have to call it quit! It was a lot colder now than it was this morning.

I got dressed and doubled check all the openings to make sure it was all air tight and walk downstairs to Frosty. I put my stuff in the saddle bags and walked back in to finish dressing quickly. I could not afford to build up sweat and go back in this cold with wet moist skin. "Not that it would be a lot more stupid than what I am doing now!!"

I took off from the Churchill Falls Hotel complex filled with mixed emotions. I could not say or pinpoint what they were but, I was sure I would find out as I moved toward the final destination. "Shit! I sound like Captain Jean-Luc Picard of the Enterprise in Star Trek!" I know for a fact that my learning is not over yet! Riding past

the Ultramar gas station for the 4th time in 4 days the guys waved at me. I waved back and got back on 500 for the last 245 kms to Labrador City!
Inside, I felt dead and disappointed to be so out of control and at the same time happy! What can I say?
I did not understand what was going on. It is as if I am fuelled by some kind of energy that is alien to me. I know damn well that if I made it here it was because of God's grace and some skills. But make no mistake? No matter what! I should not be on the road.
Where do I draw the line? I know I should have drawn it when I entered the TLH. But there was no point whining about this now.

After all, I made it to Goose Bay! This should have been enough! But NooooooH! As much as I was confused and kind of angry at myself for putting myself through this I was also in a state of absolute, pure and unadulterated joy. Did I say happy? Never mind! I have thought about this quite a bit during my Coast to Coast winter trip last year. What I learned last year as far as emotions are concerned was adding to the ones I felt this year. It was frustrating to not be able to find the words that can accurately describe this. I wish I could but I can't.

Imagine if you will a feeling, an emotion that results from putting in one pile; fear, terror, pain, discomfort whether it is emotional, physical or psychological, mixed with joy, and a sense of accomplishment, happiness about being blessed enough to do this. I suppose it is like someone who is about to take his/ her last breath and knows inside his/her heart that there is no regrets, no sorrows and nothing but the absolute conviction that the life that was lived would be lived again the same way, then take your last breath smiling. That person cannot tell you how it feels once they are gone! Well! I can't! It must absolutely be experienced. I can try and I will try many times I am sure. But I know I can't.

As I listened to Frosty rolling on the crackling snow and ice I thought of this last part from Goose Bay to

Churchill Falls and how much I was hurting and how intense it was. Now all I had to worry about was how much more I could push myself.

The River around Churchill Falls that is normally flowing wildly is peacefully sleeping without the dam working with her. Judging by the rocks and the terrain I am sure it is pretty wild when running full power.

This was awesome from the adventure point of view but it was way passed the too dangerous point.
I was trying to see if it was really just blind ego, pride or something like this but it I did not think so. Well! The hell with it! I was here now, and I would try to enjoy it no matter what.

It turns out that this decision would make the rest of the trip to Labrador City a lot more enjoyable. Focus on the positive side of this and the negative one seems to fade away. I spent the first few hours toward Labrador City thinking about this.

As I refocused I realized that I was not even noticing the scenery and could not remember what the road looked like for the whole first hour. This was nuts! No matter how bad this could get, what I was living now I couldn't relive again. The whole trip was about "firsts". If I did not bring back every memory about this, I would have taken all these chances for nothing. "So! Paul! "Stop being so fatalistic; even though there are many reasons to be, get a F^%$# hold of yourself and look the other way."

The road got darker and the air much colder with every minute the sun got lower. They had forecasted bitter cold, and the -60C they said we would have was announcing its arrival. I said that already didn't I?

The sight of this beautiful sunset on this frozen road is an awesome reminder of how blessed I am.

This will be something I will talk about for the rest of my life, and that I will take to my grave not regretting. I am sure some lessons will be painful, but in the end it will all about "Living"

The last few hours toward Labrador City went by kind of peacefully. The cold was mind numbing and again, the isolation was sobering. But taking it in one kilometre at the time for what it is took me to my destination.

The traffic increased as I got closer. Hydro trucks, big pick-ups and industrial vehicles started to appear. I can't remember ever being so happy to see humans appear like this.
There was no stinking boom box playing low riding racer look alikes baseball cap on the wrong side teenager driven Japanese P.O.S cars driving around in these parts. I saw real people! Tough ones! Hardened by the bitter cold and hard work! But make no mistake about it. Contrarily to the above mentioned morons, these guys all waved and smiled at me.

A fuel stop at the local Shell station quickly confirmed that people who live in these parts are genuine. I did not have time to gas up when a pick-up truck with the big Hewitt sign on his door stopped besides me. The driver got out and as he walked towards me said *"Man! I was coming down the road and saw you! I had to turn around to actually see it to believe it. I read about you in the North 53 magazine and heard your interview on CBC and absolutely wanted to see it firsthand. We knew you were on your way because that is all people coming off the road say"*

His name is Wayne. He runs the big Caterpillar Hewitt shop in Wabush right on the Labrador City outskirts. He offered me to keep Frosty in his warehouse for a couple days. I told him I was only here until tomorrow morning. He replied *"Oh No! It will hit -61C tomorrow and warm up to -58C the day after. They say it will hit -50 and warmer on Thursday! I think you should sit it out Paul! This is not good! Things are shutting down here!"*
I looked at the traffic going by and how all the vehicles were covered with ice and snow. But what convinced me was how everyone was dressed. No matter who sold winter clothing in here, I can guarantee you they must

carry a whole shitload of it because Furry hoods, mittens, mukluks and Heavy Duty winter suits were all I could see. I took Wayne on his offer. I followed him to his shop where he opened the huge door and steam forming as the warm inside air made contact with the brutally cold outside convinced me even more that I was making the right choice. We parked Frosty inside and I packed my belongings in his pick-up truck.

Wayne from Hewitt Caterpillar in Wabush Labrador with Frosty.
Wayne what can I say? You literally saved my skin and my ass. Your hospitality and friendship was proof of what I say of people in Newfoundland and Labrador. You redefine hospitality.

Thanks

I left Frosty in the warmth of this huge building where she looked like a toy amongst the huge machinery and engine surrounding her. But somehow I believe that she belongs with these. Great machines at work in hostile climates! Good night Frosty!

Frosty basking in warmth for a couple of days. First time she has been complete (With the sidecar) inside of a building since we left Victoria.

After making sure she was ok Wayne drove me to the Two Seasons Hotel where a shower and rest would be so welcome. Wayne asked me if I would like to join him for lunch tomorrow. He offered to come and get me whenever I would be ready, then we would go to the shop where I could look after Frosty. Once I'd be done we would go to the Hotel in the restaurant and have lunch. I thankfully accepted.

We spent time talking about bikes, travels, work and he gave me a good history lesson of how Labrador came to be and its people.

I also had to contact Mike Power. The host for CBC radio who offered me his house while I was there. We have stayed in contact since I stopped over in LC a few days ago and accepted his offer. But tonight I was too tired. I was so emotionally and physically drained that as soon as I entered my room I collapsed. I am not the friendliest person once I reach this state. Being like this around Mike would have been unfair to him and me.

I gave him a call and told him about my trip down here and he understood. When I told him that I would be staying in LC for two days he offered me to go to his house for dinner the following day, which I accepted immediately.

That night I had barely enough energy to let people know I had made it alive. I got to bed blissfully unaware that a huge storm had started brewing in my life and that all hell would break loose in a couple of days.

Good night

Day 20

January 21st 2008
Arrived in Labrador city last night at 7:30 PM
It was -50C
And Frosty hit the 30,000 km mark

It was 9:00 am when I got up. I grabbed a shower to wake up and sat down on the bed staring at the weather channel. It was -55°C (-61°F) and it was supposed to get colder by the end of the day and then warm up by tomorrow morning.

I was not going anywhere! How do you spell freaking cold? Ah yeah! H---O----L------Y   S------H------I--------T!!! That is how! I am sure you can freeze the balls of a brass monkey! I decided to not go anywhere because this was really too dangerous! Even people in here who were chatting with me said it would be too dangerous or insane (Same) to leave.

I also had to be honest about the fact that I did not know what it would do to Frosty and my organs. The day went by fairly quietly which was exactly what I needed.

Shortly after I got up Wayne came and picked me up. We drove to the Hewitt shop where I will work on Frosty a bit. I fixed the oil leak permanently. At least I thought I did! I will talk about this later. I also cleaned up all my gear and made sure that everything was working properly. As I cleaned Frosty I discovered that the steering head bearing had died. With all the shocks and vibration caused by the TLH and the corrugated ice, the bearing could not hold on. But it would have to be ok for now. Kind of hard to find a bearing here! I am also not turning the handlebars that much anyway! It will have to do. If it ever screws up to the point where it is dangerous I will deal with it then.

Once we were done we went for lunch at the Two seasons hotel restaurant. Wayne and I sat there and chatted about nothing and everything.

Once we were done Wayne went back to work and said he would pick me up tomorrow morning and take me to Frosty. Naturally I tried to pay for lunch but Wayne would not let me. I will have to buy him lunch next time I go to LC. Thanks Wayne.
The rest of the afternoon went really relaxed. I updated my blog and drank coffee while watching TV a bit.

I tried to stay away from The Weather Channel as it was or should I say had become my nemesis. I wrote some more of my personal notes and before I knew it was time for me to go to Mike's place. I called a cab and told the cab I was going to Mike Power's. He knew where it was. I guess Mike is known down there.

Mike is not only a great radio host but also a great host as well. When I got there he had the whole thing organised. Great diner, great wine, and all the things to make a guest feel at home!
Mike is not only a radio host but he is also a traveller and a superb photographer. We ended up talking about the places we had seen and he showed my some of his work. Amazing! He also gave me a picture of a Husky dog he took as he knew how much I love dogs and how much I missed mine as well.

The end of the evening came and I had to go back to the hotel and catch some ZZZ's I was determined to leave tomorrow even though it had warmed up to only about -50.
Mike was not impressed with my decision but he knew already how stubborn I am. So he wished me luck and we parted promising to staying touch.
We did as he also became part of another winter/motorcycle adventure thing. But that is another story.

January 22nd 2008
7:30 Am
Leaving Labrador City in a balmy -51°C

7:00 Am came quickly. I looked outside and it looked like frozen hell. I could hear the squeaking of the snow under the cars' tires from my room! DAMN! I got dressed and I waited for Wayne. My little angel on my right shoulder kept yelling at me to stay here and the other kept telling "Ah come on you Pansy!" This morning was one of these mornings where my pride was located in the wrong place. If I only waited till Thursday they forecast – minus 40. Much better! But NoooooH I had/wanted to go.

Wayne came and picked me up. He had trouble believing I was leaving but he still backed me up! When I got to the Cat shop they were are all there waiting for me!

Wayne and his crew at Hewitt in Wabush. Thanks Guys

Great bunch! They gave me a nice Hewitt Sticker that I promptly put on Frosty. I gave her the one and only swipe of a clean rag she will get in the whole trip. Cat Sticker! That has to make her proud and feel stronger right???

They also gave me a Caterpillar Hat and Coffee mug and thermos kit. We took picture and exchanged info and promised them that if I turned around because it was too cold or any other reason that I would come right back to the shop. The large door opened up and when I hit the cold air outside it hit me like a wall.

I stopped on the side of the road to take a picture of the moon hovering over the horizon. It was unbelievable to see it. It was surreal. It felt like I was on another planet.

Morning leaving Labrador City.

It was about four kilometres to the Two Seasons Hotel and by the time I reached it I had frost on my brows. Holy crap! What the hell was I thinking? I had promised Kathrina (The receptionist) that I would come back to see her and take pictures when she started her shift with Frosty and I. The least I can do is oblige!

We had chatted quite a bit the evening before and had a great time. Hard working local lady who gives it all she has like they all do around these parts I am sure.

Above: Frosty outside the Two Seasons Hotel

Below: Katrina and I in Labrador City

After saying my goodbyes I went to CBC radio where Mike wanted to give me another interview. This time the folks at CBC Radio in St- John's NL wanted me to compare the two highways! The one on The Rock VS the TLH.

I had to say that the TLH in winter makes the NL hwy look like kindergarten stuff. It was not meant as an offense to the road on The Rock, and I sure hope that my friends in Newfoundland will not take it personally. The reason why I think it is so much harder is the isolation.

Both are incredible. Both are in Labrador/NL; which is home to the most hospitable and friendly people in the world. We could all learn from them. So after taking a couple of pictures I took off toward Baie-Comeau! I realized pretty freaking quickly thank you very much what -51°C feels like. A layer of ice built up instantly on the inside of my visor! Somehow I thought that having the makeshift filters would take care of this problem!

It is 28 kms from Lab City to Fremont and it felts like 500! *"Oh Crap! I am not done yet!"* is what I thought.

Right away I am thinking that my decision to leave might not be a good idea! But I can hear my little devil's voice saying "Come on! You Can do it!!"

By the time I reached Fire Lake where the road criss-crosses the railroad track for about 65 kms I knew I was in for a hell of a ride. Even though my feet were not cold and neither was my body, I was already shaking. It took a while for my body to readapt after being stopped for two days! My wheels were turning, but the tires felt like they were made of metal. The Ohlin's shock felt like it was a cheap one until it warmed up. What amazed me the most was that Frosty had not broken in half already with all the pounding and shrinking metal in that cold weather?

I stopped by the mine entrance where they line the road with the big tires to protect the road (If you can call that a road!) from the wind and drifting snow.

***The road by Fire Lake Mine is lined
with huge truck tires***

As I stopped and got off the bike I realized that my suit was as stiff as a board. When I left forty minutes before it was dry but somehow it felt like the moisture in the air froze on contact and made the material feel like metal. Would be hard to take a leak! Hopefully no dump!!
After about fifteen minutes I could not see anymore. The layer of ice inside my visor was too thick. I lifted the visor to scrape it off and in about three nano-freaking seconds my eyeballs froze like marbles. Shit did this hurt.
I stopped and I put my hands in front of the muffler to warm up the gloves and hopefully this would help scrape the ice off. HMMMMM! That is not hot! I took off my glove and the exhaust was warm. So I put my hand in front of it and wrapped around it as I held my glove to warm things up a bit.
I put my glove back on and I was ok! I leaned over and directed the heat of the muffler on my closed visor! Dammit! Barely enough to make the ice melt! I scraped it again and eventually scraped it off. If I have to do this

like this till I am in Baie-Comeau I should be there by spring and will not need to do this anymore.

I came up with an idea. I took a piece of towel and stuffed it inside my tank bag! Remember the fire breathing warmer. Hopefully it would warm up the towel enough to help me wipe off the ice inside the visor as needed.
This piece of towel was wrapped around my camera. I think I heard my camera say "Es-tu fou tabarnac? Prends ta propre guenille trou du cul! Je gèle icitte aussi croupion!" Roughly translated? Take your own rag you asshole! I am freezing here too you moron!

This went on every fifteen minutes, each time I had to stop. And to make matters worse, I had the sun straight in my face! I could not see shit and there was hardly a piece of straight road! Scary! I scared myself silly or should I say shitless a few times. First! I was going down through the twisties at about 20 km/h and I could not see 10 feet ahead of me.
So I came up with a plan! A damn good one! I would lift my shield just for a second. Long enough for me to size up the road and memorize it. Then I would close the shield again because my eye balls would freeze in a second then I would navigate blind based on what I remembered of the road.

Brilliant! Abso-freaking-lutely brilliant! I could line up the bike for about 50 feet like this. And if my left wheel hit the snow bank I knew I had to turn right and if my hack wheel hit the snow bank I knew I had to steer left.
Pretty freaking tiring! To be honest with you I should have turned around right there and then!
At one point I was riding blind and something, I do not know what; but something told me to stop. I stopped and I was still on the road. But ahead of me, about fifty feet was this dark wall, and I could not quite make what it was. So I got close to about fifteen feet of it; and then I saw! It was a train! A freaking train!

You think guardian angels don't exist? Well I have news for you!

This sobered me up a bit-kind of-sort of Naaah!. By this time I knew I was doing stuff I was not supposed to do. There was no traffic and somehow I thought I could play like this. But there was rigs going on this road and I would have to come across one at one point. So I kept going hoping that my luck would hold.
A bit later I am coming on top of a crescent. Still blind, and in the curve a rig is coming. The thing is that I was in his lane. Right away I knew I could not make the turn. So I turned right and made my sidecar wheel hit the snow bank instead! This stopped my rig before the truck would even try to avoid me. I could see him because his stacks were high and I could see them coming. But he could not have seen me. This was one thing to dick around like this; but another to put them at risk like this.

"Shit! Shit! Shit! This is what my vocabulary would dwindle down to for the next 8 to 10 hours on my way to Baie-Comeau!
I got off the bike again and performed my half ass defrosting circus dance again! By this time I had started my frozen bacon dance as well!
I took off again! The wind picked up, the drifting snow was blinding me most of the time.
All that was happening on a road where one needs 100% of your vision. By this time my eyes were hurting and watering, my face was burning and I was freaked. But being the way I am I kept going! Why not push it all the way.
I had only about 100 kms done by that this time and I could have turned around! But nope!
A bit later I was in a curve and right in front of me was a rig in my lane! He had no choice! The road was narrow and he could not see me coming. I was lower than the snow banks. Plus; I was the last thing he expected. I saw his hands turn the steering wheel to the left and I cleared the tractor. But I had another 53 feet of the 40

tons rig coming toward me and it looked like we are about to make contact. I slide my rig's rear end away from him and then gunned it! It pulled me away from the rig but in the opposite direction I was supposed to turn. I was thinking *"I will be ok if I hit the snow bank!"* So far so good my front end was clearing him! I thought! I could see his wheels sliding as well, and I was sure he was hoping as hard as I was! As the rear end of the trailer was going by me I was squinting and going "OHHHHHHH SHIIIIIIIIIITTTTTT!" and I skimmed the tail end of it! I shit you not there was not enough room between his trailer and my handlebar to slide an ass hair. I know I could feel every strand of hair straightening and every muscle pucker in a moment like this. Pucker factor of 9.89 out of 10 aside! This was too much! I stopped when I could on the side and walked around a bit.

After about 5 minutes of talking to myself, I kept on going. So far so good! 120 kms out of 270 clicks to Relais Gabriel! And another 240 to Baie-Comeau, and so far I have almost died at least 3 times.

I was losing my sight, my nerves were shut, my body felt like it was carrying about three tons, and my mind was laughing at me. Please God let me make it to Relais Gabriel!

By the time I reached it I was beyond exhausted I have ever felt! I fuelled Frosty and then wobbled my way in the restaurant in the Pourvoirie/hotel where folks remembered me and were happy to see I made it. No one was freaking happier than me at that point.

I should have rented a room right there but the adrenaline rush was taking control of my senses. It was really intense and fun in some way. Logic was not even part of the equation anymore and risk was nothing but a word hard to pronounce when you are shivering with fear.

Years ago I jumped out of a deuce and a half at 60 MPH while I was on an exercise with the army because I did not want to be in the field for three months. I preferred the idea of a broken leg than the idea of living in mud and tranches for three months. Well I did not break a damn thing and I stayed there! This was one of my memorable stupid moves in my life that I will always cherish as a major DUH moment. And as dumb as it was it was smarter than what I was doing today.

I ordered a bowl of soup and a sandwich and slowly stopped climbed back down from the high. As I sat there chatting with the waitress I felt my neck hurting big time. I touched it and felt some kind of thick hard patch on my throat! I went in the can to look in the mirror and saw I had a real bad frostbite right on my Adam's apple! It was obvious I had not closed the storm flap properly on my suit and the cold wind made it in. The frostbite had the shape of the zipper slider. Almost 2 years later as I write this I still have marks on my neck reminding me how lucky I am to be here today being able to talk about it.

Anyway! I spent about an hour in Relais Gabriel and I put on one more pair of socks and one more layer on top. The guys who operate the grader between mile marker 200 and 253 took a picture of me again. Now they knew I was nuts! It was a bit warmer in here. The temp had gone down to about -30 something. Not bad! So I decided to try to make it to Manic 5 Motel de l'Energie where I'd fuel up and hopefully take off and make it to Baie-Comeau.

By the time I reached Manic 5 I could hardly see, my face was burnt and I was so tense I could hardly get off Frosty. When I walked in and people saw my face they stopped talking. My skin was red as a berry and looked burnt.

In the cafeteria was a bunch of truckers who told me that they were all following me and that they knew at all times where I was! They took pictures of me as I went by. Hydro Quebec, TELUS, and other workers were there as well. There must have been forty people in there, and we all sat close to each other, talked, joked and laughed.

This was the medicine I needed. After a good serving of soup and a good serving of laughter I handed out about forty of my business cards with my address and info. Amazing what a good serving of road camaraderie, a plate of laughter topped off with a thick layer of care can do. I made my way out to Frosty ready for the last stretch. By the time I was back on the road I was starting to talk to myself again most of the time.

Pep talk I guess! The road was dark and lonely. The sun had gone down and I knew I had another three hours to Baie-Comeau where a bed in Los Tabarnacos' house was waiting for me! At times I was not sure if I would make it or not. My mind was storming colisse!!

The road was rough beyond anything I had ever done. Every bump sent a radiating pain down my back. My back was in so much pain I knew that I could not get off my bike anymore. All I could do was wiggle a bit; suck in my abdominal muscles for a few seconds to alleviate the pressure off my spine and keep going.
Rene (Los Tabarnacos) had asked me to send a "I am OK" signal off my Spot GPS Tracker when I would reach Manic 2, so he could meet me at the Labrador road entrance and escort me home. I sure hoped he would be there because I was so done for I knew I could not find my way to his house. I would have to stop at a gas station somewhere and ask for help..
One kilometre at the time I was getting closer to the end. By the time I have about 100 kilometres left to go, it was a battle of the mind over the body!

Anyone who knows me will tell you that I can take pain. And I can heal from anything very quickly. By the time 6 rolled in I was not even sure anymore if I would make it the next one hundred yards; let alone healing.

I had started to cry a little while ago and at times I had to stop, move around on the bike and wiggle any part that could be wiggled, and wipe y tears off my mask as they froze on the baklava. At one point I took my helmet off in the middle of nowhere to shock me and the ice pulled my hair off my face as all of this was one frozen mess. After about 5 minutes on the bike with no helmet, I had to put it back on. This rest lasted for about ten minutes and I started balling again.

I had reached my limits and anything past this was new territory for me.

I could feel my body slowly shutting down! I could feel my guts cooling off! This was not good because in times of cold and stress the body redirects all blood flow to the core for the organs to function. My feet and fingers were not frozen but they were numb. The exhaustion finally got to me.

By then I had about an hour to go and it was hard to keep telling myself "Come on Paul! You can make it! "Don't you dare give up on me you piece of shit! Not now! Wait! Hang on! You did not make it this f%$#@ far to be found an hour away from your goal!

I arrived in Baie-Comeau on 22 January at 30603 km at 8:00 PM beyond exhausted

I know it sounds foolish and some (Macho) guys would not say this; but I could not stop crying. If someone had heard me as they went by they would have forced me to stop. I finally made it to the intersection of 389 where Rene was! He saw quickly how burnt out I was as I was crying and barely hanging on the bike and that we had to go home now!

He said "Hold on a bit longer buddy! We are almost there! (Shit I am crying as I write this! The feeling is still so intense) When I got close to Rene's place there was a police cruiser with his siren on behind me! I thought *"F^%$# this! I am too tired to deal with this!"* and I kept going a couple of blocks till I got to Rene's.

I turned off Frosty. Collapsed on the tank bag and sobbed like a baby. I was shaking, shivering out of control.

This lasted about 5- 10 minutes while Rene was talking to the police officers who were two young officers. Nice guys! They were just wondering about this nut out here in the cold at night.

When I got off Frosty I could not climb the stairs I was in such pain! I made it in and Rene took my boots off. I sat in the stairs and fell on my back in the entrance way with my back in the snow and THAT IS ALL SHE WROTE!

Too burnt out to take my own boots off. But man was I happy to be there and out of the TLH

I stayed up for an hour having nice hot coffee and out in the coma I went. I will write about my trip to Joliette later. One word of advice! You want to do this trip in winter????? Don't!

Iceman out!

January 23rd 2008
Baie-Comeau Quebec

What follows was what should have been in the medical paper the day after I got out of the TLH.

The Baie-Comeau medical journal has documented what is believed to be the world's first case of resurrection.
On the evening of January 22nd 2008 after coming back from what is considered and impossibly cold accomplishment, riding the Labrador Highway in winter on a motorcycle from Baie-Comeau to Goose Bay and back in temperatures that hovered for a couple of days around -55C, Mr Paul Mondor also known to many as "Iceman" approached his bed at the residence of Mr Rene Roy at around 10 PM and is believed to have fallen asleep before his body actually hit the hay. With the help of sonic analysis technology and infra red graphic display instrumentation the witness to this event (The owners of the house) confirmed that indeed Iceman had lost consciousness before touching his mattress. To further the proof, the loud sonic emanation coming out of Iceman as well as his face who splattered on the pillow like a blob of pudding dumped on any surface were accompanied by spasms and unrecognisable sounds. After a few seconds of this, all brain activities stopped as Iceman stopped moving and breathing (Some argue this is Apnoea!)
The drooling that followed and the motionlessness suggested that indeed death had occurred. According to witnesses at around 8 AM Iceman for some unknown to the medical and scientific community came back to life as his brain sent an electric impulse signal to brain making it say "Heeey Colisse que j'ai dormi? J'penses que chu mort pendant 8 heures!"

Translation: Hey for Fu$#%^' sake'! Did I ever sleep! I think I died for 8 hours!

This also vigorously brought back in the debate between the medical and scientific community, the topic and age old argument as whether or not the brain or part of it is still functioning during death's occurrence!

Evidence of that was gathered in the room where Iceman was sleeping by the owners as they were making the bed. Quote: "Apparently he did die according to the smell of flatulencies in here strong enough to peel the paint off the wall! End quote. Strengthening even more the theory that the human brain can indeed sustain bowel and gas functions in times of complete shut down!

I got up at "What the hell thirty. Don't know! My brain was still on the pillow.
I got up at 8:00 to get ready and go! But first things first and I let Los Tabarnacos know that WE were having breakfast at Tim Horton's and that I would leave from there!
After a good breakfast and a good cup of black plasma I suited up, said goodbye to Rene and headed down the road. Even though the road was a lot nicer than what I had been on for the last five days, what made it easier was that it was a balmy -20C. Yoo Hoo! Finally! Spring weather! There was obviously more snow around now than there was when I came by, which told me that after all, weather wise speaking; the weather was following me just like last year! Might just be my colisse de paranoia?? (I am French! What's your excuse?) Anyways! As soon as I got to Outardes the wind joined me in my trek. But????? It had decided it was going the other way! In these parts of PQ the altitude is like the possibility of a politician screwing you. It goes up and down but mainly stays up. And at times my speed went down to 30 km/h. The roads were clear in some parts and in others the snow drifts covered the whole road.

I was keeping an eye on Frosty as she was losing quite a bit of oil through the air box and vents. No damage though! And she was still purring. But I made sure the oil level remained high enough. The vibration caused by the sprocket crown bearing going into retirement stayed the same the same and I kept an eye on this too!
That was the only thing the TLH had damaged. Considering the savage beating Frosty had taken for over 1200 kilometres of the TLH; which had been so much harder than the rest of the rest, she was doing unbelievably well!
Nothing so far had broken! Like I said before; I am convinced that NO OTHER bike would/could have done this and survived. I was sad to think that they would not make the 650 GS anymore. I know that this was their (BMW) best bike. I have had all of their models and I can tell you that I am trimming my stable down to one bike and it is Frosty. You'd have an impossible time trying or even dreaming to convince me or others who have travelled on the 650 singles that more is better.
I have crossed the country twice on my faithful Frosty and in conditions that were insanely hard on a piece of hardware. And I have done many other long trips on her.
Except for riding at 120 mph all day, there is nothing she cannot do that the big adventures do! I know, I have of these too. Ok enough of this. You know now how I feel about the singles
Back to the trip to Joliette! The trip to the Tadoussac ferry was a mix of high winds, hills, snow drifts and covered roads in higher altitudes. When I got on the ferry there was a bunch of sledders there as well. I rode past them on Frosty and it was funny to look at the whole scene. Motorcycles and snowmobiles together, waiting to go on the ferry.

Without getting into details I can tell you that their display of manhood got seriously dampened by the arrival of a little 650 cc motorcycle in their winter world. You know how as motorcyclists we all interact with others? Well the same thing goes for sledders! But these guys would not even approach me. I nodded at a couple of them but judging by their reaction I was the scum of the earth. At least that is what it felt like.

Maybe it had something to do with someone (Not me) saying *"Man that was funny! I was parked beside them as you were coming down the hill toward the ferry and they literally quieted down when they saw you, and went back to their machines. Suddenly their "We own our winter land" behaviour disappeared, and they walked away!"* They heard this fellow say this to me on the boat and that was it! Well you know? It was funny in a "You had to be there" way.

Frosty and the sleds

Welcome to Quebec winters

After pictures were taken, addresses exchanged and hands shaken with the fellows parked behind Frosty, we all parted when the ferry docked, and I kept on going.
The weather got progressively worse as I crossed little village after another. But the scenery was nice when the weather would break and give me a chance to enjoy the scenery.

When I hit Baie St-Paul; that was it! Winter was in full gear. Nothing but wind, snow and drifting squalling white stuff everywhere, but I was enjoying it. I guess that with all the people around I was not reacting to the conditions the same way I had in the past week.

As I went up the hill coming out of Baie St-Paul the snow was everywhere. Traffic had really slowed down and it got slipperier.

I went up and across these parts at about 60 clicks and just scooted along.

When I got to the downhill side of it coming into St-Anne de Beaupre it was pretty much the same, and it stayed this way as I went across Beauport, Quebec and through Donnacona and Trois-Rivières.

I stopped for about half an hour in Louiseville at La Porte de la Mauricie. This is a stop area/truck stop I stopped at many times in my trucking years, and foolishly enough I willingly took ten years of my life by having an A&W chicken sandwich.

This tasted good, but I always wonder if what they serve is really coming from anything that was once part of the animal kingdom!

I always say *"I do not mind eating anything that had a face or a mother"* but I am sure if you read what these places put in their sandwiches, there are very few if any ingredients which name does not have numbers in it.

You see stuff like Water, aqua, sugar and preservatives and then stuff like Holycrapnite 259, livakilla136, stronggasite378 and whatdafukarium2098.

I cannot remember the last time I ate in a fast food burger joint. Probably has something to do with the time when I was trucking and stopped at one of these service plazas along 401 and bough two Burger King© burgers. One for me and one for my Dog Breaker (Bless her soul! I still cry when I think about her!)

As I ate my burger she was sitting on the double bunk in the sleeper in front of the burger, looked at it, walked away and laid down in the back.

To make a long story short, thirty minutes later, I had to call dispatch and ask them to send a driver.

My girlfriend at the time drove 500 kilometres to come and get me. After going to the hospital, I found out I had food poisoning!

Here is a hint! Give a bite of whatever you are about to eat to your loving dog, and if he does not eat it you should not either.
Anyways! After this culinary wonder I made to my mom's house where she almost got into complete cardiac arrest as she saw me walking up the stairs and knocking on her door! I guess once a mom always a mom! She does not care if I am 2 or 47! I am still her little boy!

Had coffee at mom's and then went to my brother's where they were waiting and very happy to see me in one piece.
 I spent about an hour up (At least trying) and then I hit the hay. I had asked Bruno not to wake me up and let me sleep. I had to catch up. This was the first time in 3 weeks where I felt I did not have a schedule to follow and it was great!

I took a few condensed notes and went to bed.
Arrived in Joliette at 31 234 km at 9 PM on January 23 2008

Iceman out tabarnac!!!!

Day 23

January 24th Joliette Quebec
Home for a few days due to Frosty and I needing TLC.

On my way down to Joliette I had made a phone call and asked JJ if he could help me with schedule some work done on Frosty at Monette Sports in Laval Quebec.
Being the man and friend he is it was done in no time. Frosty needed a tune up, oil and filters.
I called for a plate form truck to come and pick her up and they showed up the day after.

Frosty was on her way to get some TLC from BMW. Meanwhile I would get my own

Meanwhile I needed my own TLC too. While I was in Baie-Comeau two nights ago I found out that Melanie had decided to dump my ass. She needed to figure out who I was and what kind of man I was. I guess she could not understand anymore while I would put myself and those I love through this.

Here she was with all her panels gone, ready to be worked on. It is as if I could hear her giggle with relief

It really hit me hard. Actually I kind of lost my freaking mind. What had been an incredible adventure was now just a thing that was costing me a lot. I remember reading Ted Simon's book (Dreaming of Jupiter) and asking why he would jeopardize his world trip and dreams for the sake of someone. I know! I know! Sounds selfish of me!
It looked as if suddenly his whole ability to focus evolved around the woman he thought he loved.
I know Bla! Bla! Bla! You are right! Anyway!
I was hurting, I was lost and I did not know what to do. All I knew was that I was going to a roommate not the partner I had left 3 weeks ago.

I ended up writing my heart out and tried to sort things out.

Ok! Time to cut the crap!

We have been a hell of a ride! It has been fun and it has been hard! There are few things I have been told and I will quote!
"You brought people together"
"We lived the ride through you!"
You have a skill at allowing others to live your own emotions!"
For these things, I am thankful! But what I want to write now has nothing to do with all this. And it WILL be the last entry! As it has always been, I have learned and am learning as we speak a hell of a lesson! And I am learning it the hard way.
Let's rewind here to the day I came back to Baie-Comeau. That night was the accumulation of things that rank in the hardest I have ever done! To say the TLH scared the hell out of me, that it was so much harder than I had anticipated and that it through curves at me that I was NOT prepared for would not only be an understatement but a hell of a lie! Behind all these tabarnacs and colisses was a guy who was really lost.
That night when I called Melanie she told me that she did not understand why I was pushing myself like this and putting myself through this. I tried to explain as we all remember that it was the need to feel to the extreme and to be

reminded how precious life was. This is all good and nice! A guy leaves pushes himself to the absolute limits and dies on the side of the road. Not married, with no one and no responsibilities, nothing and no one will really miss him. This is not my case! Never was!

And I am thankful it will never be! Well I hope not! I was also told that I could come back someone different and by the grace of God I have! But in a good way! While I was gone something happened! It might not be the trip, and then it might be. One thing is for sure this tri has started a chain of events that has caused me in the last 24 hours to have the biggest examination of my own heart and soul. The real reason I did this is that till yesterday I had no freaking idea and only made myself believe things.

Now hurting like I am hurting I can say it is pride and ego that were my fuel. And to add to the mixture they were really well misplaced. I knew I could handle the trip but I knew the TLH would be more than I could handle. Being the man I am and I will simply say "Being a man!" It was impossible for me (At that time) to admit that to myself out loud, let alone to others.

After all I am Iceman right?

What I should have done is go to the ones I love

and who are close to me. (You can all; at least I hope, relate to this), and said "Ok! I am worried here! And yes I am scared! I thought I could do the TLH and I was wrong! And not only this, but I also know that it would not only put myself at risk but the wellbeing of others! Like you Melanie! Like Travis, Amber, and my friends and all the others who care for me! I do not know how to stop this!"
But I did not! I swallowed hard and held on to the belief that if I did not go through with the plan I would be a failure. That I would be looked at as someone who chickened out and did not have the strength to proceed! And off I went! The trip across was ok till I hit the TLH. Then all hell broke loose!

Well! Let me tell you this! I have failed! I have failed miserably not as a rider but as a man! As a friend, as a partner and lover, also has a brother, uncle, son, cousin and might have you! Now I am a day away from flying home! Frosty just came in! She is good and was ok all the time! But I could not give a shit less! Let me explain! I know some of you out there personally. I know you as friends and riders in adventure. But those of you I got to know personally, I also got to know as dads, moms, brothers, sisters, boyfriends and girlfriends.

And from what I have seen I know that none of you would put yourself at risk like this. Not because you are scared of doing the ride! No! Not because you do not have the skills! No! But simply because you could not and would not put your loved ones through this!

As simple as that! And in this there is no failure! There is no shame! And there is no loss! Looking back, the last 2 years have been dedicated to these trips. 2 F%^$#* years! I have been blessed with Melanie and her kids for almost 3 years now! And in this there is pride, a sense of accomplishment and a total and undeniable success!

While I was busy dreaming, boasting myself and lining up these trips, especially this last one, pride and ego grew. The last one was ok! It was ok only in retrospective! Because compared to this one, there were no risk and it was a walk in the park.

When I came back last year it was total absolute celebration. And relief was in the air. This year felt like this till I came back to Baie-Comeau. And my writings about it like I said brought me to this day. Today! I am sitting here with my eyes so full of tears by the time I will be done it will have taken me 2 hours to write this.

I have written that I felt like I have failed by not

coming back on 2 wheels!! In fact I have failed because I just found out how much I have hurt Melanie and those close to me. I scared them! I got them so scared to lose me that a lot has taken place. It will be my job from now on to fix this and make sure it will never happen again! I have never really asked for anything but I am now! I am asking the big guy up there to allow me to go back home Wednesday night and mend the damage the last 2 years have done. Like I said; especially this last one.

I have romanticized and glamorized the whole thing. I am not taking away what I have done! What I hate right now is the result and the reason why I was not able to draw the line between calculated risk adventure and heart stopping fear, pointless risks that could have cost so much to those who mean so much to me.

Ron, Doug, Kevin, Steve, Geoff, Woodgrain, THM, Lornce, and all the others I ask you this not as riders but as men! How far would you go before you risk too much and see, really see what and who you must stop this nonsense for?

My good friend Rob in Vancouver said this and I quote "You of course are most welcome to ride with us. Since I am a chicken, I will have a backup SUV with satellite phone and survival gear. I have kids, so my adventures need to have

a greater safety margin."
I have shared my dreams, my joy, my pain, my fears and goals with my family of riders and I got into it so much that I actually got to believe the romanticized reality. I am not writing this to seek credit, admiration or to feed my misplaced ego and pride as a man.

I am writing this because I am going nuts, I am hurting like I never did and as usual I love to write. I also clear my mind as I do this and those of you who know me will go! "Holy Shit man! I have never heard him say this before! This is serious shit! This is not about, adrenaline, it is not about testosterones, and it is not about a plaque on the wall or a pile of newspapers to look at once in a while.
This is about Paul Mondor! Not Iceman! Just plain Paul Mondor! I know some of you will go on and say "There we go! He lost it!" others will say Ahhh! Fucking whimp! And other God knows what!

And like Gone with the wind's famous line goes! "Frankly my dear, I do not give a damn!"
No! Today is about a ride I am about to go on! And to be honest with you, THIS WILL be the hardest I have ever been on! A flight home, that will take me 3000 miles away in comfort and warmth to one of the most beautiful place on

earth. But at the end of the line lies the biggest challenge this man has ever faced.

The heart mine has been beating for, has been crippled in the way it feels for mine! And I am scared! I am hurt and the only thing I have in common with the name Iceman is because my heart and soul are frozen and paralyzed in fear! And because I feel so cold right now I do not care about anything else but what it is I can do to get this warmth back.. I have caused hurt and pain selfishly and blindly! I have ignored and I dreamed so much that I have forgotten my own reality.

I have pretended, I have lied and I have pushed aside the real feelings a real man shows in time of challenge.

I can stand anywhere in this F%^$# country and say I have conquered it twice! In winter! I have done what no one else has done! A total of over 17000 kms of frozen country!

But today I am paralyzed because the road between our hearts has frozen solid and I do not know if I can ride it. I could not see the warmth that was in my heart and arms. I was too busy looking at endless ice. Now I feel like I cannot thaw out anymore! I went too far! So let's forget about wheels and engines for now. Let's forget about rides, challenges and credit. Let's forget about who did the most and the fastest with the most power in the thickest dirt with the least *worries. Let's forget about the grunts and the cheers and the clapping which I assure you I appreciated. But right now it weighs little in the scale of life. It is about what really counts. Without people close to us sharing our dreams they mean nothing. And if you push to far your dreams might/will take away the only ones you love (d) to share them with. Then what???*

Iceman (Whatever) out

As you can see the emotions were flying high and I was in a hell of a mess. After some rest and some talk things got back to normal and I learned a thing or two about myself. But then I could really not think straight. Meanwhile I had received a call from Monette Sports and what was supposed to be a few days repair looked like maybe a week or two. The shop floor was being poured and the none of the work space and tools were available.

Something to do with them not working on bike too much in January! Go figure!
Some of the parts needed to be ordered in. The steering head bearings on Frosty had literally been cut I half by the constant pounding of the TLH and the lateral pull of the sidecar.
The rubber dampers for the rear sprockets had disintegrated and the wheel bearing were shot!
Besides this the engine was low in oil bit was running great. They had done a compression test and she was strong. The frame, electrics and everything else was fine. Like I said-considering the hell she went through she was fine.

I wrote a little something about Frosty and put it on the web. It was my way to let people know how much I loved this little bike.

Here it is

Frosty

The little one that was put in my face.

December 2006. I had been planning the first Cross Canada trip for close to a year now and this was from the beginning just a ride! After all as a motorcyclist it is riding on 2 wheels that counts. 2, solid reliable wheels. I had X amount of $$$ set aside for this trip and I had chosen a 2003 KLR 650 with only 17000 on it. It was in pristine condition and the owner was a good friend of mine. So I bought it and prepped it. I always loved the 650 Dakar. It was to me a great bike. I had owned a 2004 that got written off when a driver decided to turn left into me and use me as a 250 lbs launch able potato. Anyway I knew they were great.
But! I had a problem with tossing a 12000.00 (With all the equipment) bike in this salty frozen mess. 4 days before D-Day, we got a call from Norm Wells, president of BMW Canada saying that he will do pretty much anything to make me take off on a BMW. After all it is who I was working for.

Sitting in the corner was a 2007 BMW F650 GS Dakar. She was the last one and because the season was over on Vancouver Island she was to spend the rest of the winter sitting on the floor with some of her siblings who just like did not make the cut.

I said to Norm "How about this 2007 Dakar?" to make a long story short he said "She is yours! Go and have fun!" Four days to prep her! Change tires to TKC's, put guards on her, update fasteners to SS ones, break her in and do a shakedown run. This was a task that was big! Too fast and it was a lot to expect from me and also her. But we went for it.

In the back she went! On the lift and we started right away to remove parts and installing others etc. there was something about her! Don't know what but I have it on video as the guys are working on her. I had not ridden her yet and I was already attaching myself to her.
A whole day she spent on the lift and then she came out. 3 days we had to acquaint each other before we had to go. You al know what she went through on this first trip. She did not miss a beat! Not one! I was impressed! She came back home a month after me from Newfoundland where she was resting and also being prepared to come home. My Newfoundland cavalry took good

care of her. She came home and I spent 3 days cleaning her. But she came through shining like a little star. She spent the summer going all over and doing what she liked in temperatures she was designed for. I learned a lot on that trip and I know in some kind of way she did too. Then this trip came! She was ready and willing! Prepped even more than last year! And this year I even attached a 200lbs appendage to her without even asking her. That is half her weight. She would have to pull sideways for over 8500 kms of frozen land.

This was a lot to ask of her. I think she adapted to this sidecar thing a lot quicker than I did! As a matter of fact she adapted to it right way and I never did! I am a 2 wheel creature. Not 3! I am sure that she did not like it and had probably by then memorised all the French swear words and thrown then at me. The sidecar was a tool to me and to her it was a growth she could not shake loose.

She pulled and slid and climbed and forced every bolt in her to be tested. As the mileage piled up she hung on. The toll was high on her as far as her chain and sprockets were concerned. But I am sure that just like the infantry man on the front line, losing a finger in a life threatening battle was of little concern. I am still convinced I could hear her breathe and talk to me. And when I parked her at the end of each day in the cold night air that I was running away from myself, I would look at her and feel her clamped herself down for the night like a horse at the end of the day. Breathing, moving, aching and yet knowing full well that it had to start all over again in the morning. Every morning I walked to her and before I started her I touched her head (Dash) and asked her to hold on one more day! As I wiped the frost and ice off her seat and lights, I know she was bracing for another day. But yet, was faithfully getting up and started every time like she always had.

As always I thanked her and let her warm up. I packed her up and another day started. Day after day after day, cold frozen mile after cold frozen mile she kept on soldiering on. Each bump on the road causing her to pry her bones sideways as the sidecar required.

Then the TLH came!

We stopped at the manic 2 and took a picture of her. She was standing there, breathing and living. I know that! Just waiting for me to get over my prideful moment and allow her to move so her parts would not freeze. Thump! Thump! Thump! Thump! In an endless rhythm she sang to me. And down the road she went. This road is hard, incredibly hard on bikes in summer. Frames have broken right off, new shocks gave in, tires blew and welds came apart. In winter it is 50 times harder. Her metal was shrinking in this cold climate. Her tolerances were annihilated and things were coming lose. Small things, light cover, signals, but never a vital part. Plus she had that big ugly thing putting enormous amount of sheer lateral stress on her and she still held on. 1200 kms of bone crushing, metal bending washboards and body ripping impacts. Kilometre after kilometre she went on. And to honest with you I was amazed at how solid and sturdy this little bike has been! At times, when I was stopped and hurting in the cold hard night, I knew I was in that mess because of my own sheer stupidity.

I am hurting still, and writing about Frosty helps a bit. In those moments I can still see her, standing there idling at -55C with thick smoke/condensation coming out of her and for most of the trip back home, pouring oil like a deep would pour blood. It was not fatal but she had trouble breathing and exhaling. Her one and only little piston had no way of exhaling because ice kept building up in her air box. She had no choice but to vent through her head and letting go of some of her life preserving oil at every stroke. But I kept putting some in and she kept on going. At every bump that sent my spine into shock I could feel the deep impact on her. And this, repeatedly like a machine gun! It was

horrifyingly painful for me at times and still is. But there she was! As I was breathing air through the little slit in my helmet, the air at -55 was freezing my lungs almost solid and hurt in ways I had never experienced. It also was hitting my eyeballs with pain just like I had 1000's of needles thrown into them.
I am sure that is how she felt too. She ran all day. Minute after minute! When I stopped for breaks or resuscitation, she was running and stopped only at night to be abandoned in the cold again.

I can only say this now! I made it though only because of God's grace! Make no mistake about this! I have hurt in ways I never want to hurt again! Never! With a tabarnac de big capital "N" and I KNOW he brought me back home to heal. But make absolutely no mistake about this. He brought me back home on Frosty.

And I know that for 1200 kms, my so called perceived safety never or hardly existed. But the little I had rested a 100% in little 650 cc heart. She made it! And she made it back home pretty much in perfect shape except for a really screwed steering head bearing (Thanks to the sidecar) and only one litre of oil left in her.
They cleaned her up and brought her back to me. And guess what? I was obviously very

emotional and drained still when they dropped her off in my brother's driveway. But when the guy left, I sat on her, put the key in and started her. I know if I could have heard her speak she would have said "Ok Paul! I am ready! Let's go home!"

But I was not! As she started and hummed like a gentle honey bee, I cried! I really freaking did! Maudit tabarnac! Talk about a 250 lbs piece of sensitive shit! But hey! That is who I am! I hunched over her, wrapped her with my arms and hands and said "Thanks for bringing me back home!"

I will pick her up and we will ride again! She will bring me home again one more time. But this time! Make no colisse de mistake about it! It will be in a green luscious, environment!

I rode 1.3 million clicks on bikes in my life, I have owned close to 17 bikes, I have ridden incredible roads and pushed bikes to their limits more often than I care to remember. But out of all these, only one has come out brighter and shinier than any other. And only one attached itself to my heart closely and in many ways intimately. And most amazingly it is the one I have beaten the most. I can only say 2 things. First! No other bike would have survived what she did unscathed! NO OTHER. I would like to dare anyone to prove me wrong. But I will not! She *proved it and we all know it. Many had doubted her in the first trip and she came home laughing at them. Then! She survived the second trip in an even more hostile environment!*

Second? It is very simple! I could not have made it without her!

So here is to you Frosty! My close and faithful riding machine!

Thank you!

I was starting to worry. Two weeks was too long to stay out of the cold. There was no way I could get back on the road and be safe again after that. So the thought of riding back home was fading away, and with that came the disappointment. I was sad, angry and frustrated.
Looking back it is obvious that I was too tired and could not process my emotions properly. I know many people who have pushed the envelope way more than they ever had who felt the same way after their accomplishments.

After about a week I decided I would be flying home. In many ways this was better and also much safer.
I would have to wait for Frosty to come back from the shop and then I would fly out. I wanted to leave her at Bruno's and fly back in May to ride her back to BC.
Without the hack though! I was done with the hack.
I'd try to sell it and find it a good home.

I spent the last few days in Joliette resting and cleaning up. This trip had been THE trip of a lifetime. I had finally found my limits (For now?), and in the process, I unfortunately found the limits of the ones close to me.

The return back home was hard and the following two months were even harder. *"Life is not easy! Wear a helmet!"*

I had some damage control to do. Over time things went back to normal. I also promised myself and others that I would not do something like this ever again.
I had succeeded once and was not willing to find out if I could do it twice.
As I write this the Frozen Butt Tour is coming. I am taking seven riders from Baie-Comeau Quebec to Goose Bay Labrador in February 2010.
They trust me to be able to take them through this journey and they are paying me for this. I am truly blessed to have been able to do this and to also be able to help others understand end experience firsthand what riding Labrador in winter on motorcycle.

While I was home I also tended some of the wounds in my life. Some I cannot do a damn thing about and will have to let it heal and scar the way it wants too.

I could go on and on babbling and babbling and it would not change a damn thing. I am proud of what I did. Not in a boastful way but in a thankful way. I am thankful for being the way I am and being able to do stuff like this. I have made friends again that will last a lifetime and this alone is worth doing the trip.
I also made some others mad and angered some. What can I say? I was not put on this earth to win a popularity contest. I have ruffled the feelings of some naysayers and I wish I could say sorry. NOT!!!!! If some of you want to kick my ass all I can say is this. `Take a number and wait." There are many people waiting their turn.

Sitting in the plane by the window I remembered how I felt the year before when I left St-John's Newfoundland. I felt devastated and out of sort. I could not let it go and I was leaving a big part of me on the road. Now it was different. I was still exhausted and already missing the road, but I was happy to see it end in some way too.

So much had been put at stake and so many chances had been taken. The risks were insane and the danger was more than words can say. And because of this I was happy to say it was done.

There was one more thing I was happy about too. I was bringing back with me the little boy my dad had raised.

And finally, I am happy to be here writing this and not being found frozen stiff in a dead caribou's ass.

Iceman

Prologue

Not bad I guess! I often say *"Any day above ground is a good day!"*
So all in all I guess I had had a good one!
Close to nine thousand kilometres crossing Canada (Again) in winter, riding through record temperatures that reached -61°C, came close to death at least five times. Three of these were of my own choice just temporarily giving up lying down on a snow bank.

I saw Labrador in winter like no other had ever seen it in winter. From a motorcycle! The memories will stay with me forever. I still have the scars on my neck two years later from the frost bites. And thanks to God I have no permanent damage.
I am sure though that some would love to argue whether or not my brain was damaged. Moving on!

The lessons I have learned are still being processed today.

Life is short!
Friends are precious!
Fear can be conquered!
Never surrender to others' fear!
Live like tomorrow will never come!

But most importantly love what you do.

And oh yeah! I said before I was happy I found the little boy I am again, but I have to add this before I go.
I sure hope it will take a few years before I lose him again. And to be honest, I hope that if I do; that it will be in a warm place.

Go out and ride

Iceman

Thanks and acknowledgments

I will start with the One that deserves my thanks the most first. God! The Big Guy! The main Dude! Call him whatever you want; but tome he is the only reasons why I am not looking at flowers from the roots' side.

Dad! Again, there is nothing I can say that has not been said already. Without the values you gave me I would not be who I am! Thanks! I love you and there is not a day that goes by that I do not miss you.

Mom! Same thing! Without you I would not be on this planet! Not Crypton, fer crissesakes! Thanks!

To my brother Bruno, his wife Josee and my nephew and niece Patrick and Stephanie I say thanks and love you. You are my family and I am blessed to have you.

Melanie! I say it to you every day! You rock my world To my friends for STILL loving me, even though sometimes I can be like the turd that just won't flush. I love you all.

Harry Harding! Harry our friendship was forged from the get go on trust and honesty. I consider myself privileged to be able to call you "My friend" and your friendship is something I will never take for granted. Thank you for your trust and your strength. We conquered BC, Alberta, Saskatchewan and Manitoba in winter on motorcycles, and no one else can say this. What you and I have and accomplished is unique. You da Man!

To BMW, and especially John Johnston. Man! I owe you so many Snickers shooters (Don't ask!) it is not even funny!

Toronto BMW for taking care of Frosty and I the way they did. You guys are scholars and appreciate the extra mile you went for us.

Tim and Christina in Toronto. Thank you for your hospitality, but most importantly thank you for your friendship. 3000 miles separate us but you are in my thought always. Hope Junior is well too

Wayne in Wabush
Wayne and his crew took me in and Frosty and gave us shelter when Labrador was at its worst. You kept her warm and you welcomed me in like a friend. Thank you! You guys' hearts are as big as the machinery you work on.

Mike Powers in Labrador City
Thanks mike for diner and your friendship and also for your incredible culinary delights. It was damn fine

Kathrina at the Two Seasons Inn in Labrador City
What can I say? You gave a stranger a sense of being home and you welcomed us on behalf of Labrador City

Rene (Los Tabarnacos) in Baie-Comeau
Rene you are a great friend, a great host and a damn good organiser. A great thanks to your wife too. Man! How come you don't weight 500 lbs with her being that great of a cook?

Ron (ZZRon) in Dryden
Ron you are as part of these trips as Frosty was. You have been since the beginning a great friend and I am thankful for all you do, did and knowing you will do for me. Stopping in Dryden in any season would not be the same without you

To all the others I met along the way and have made this trip what it is I say thanks! I said it before and I still say it. The memories of the trip might fail one day but the people I met will always be in my mind and heart.

Night riding basic rules

1-Slow down. It is safer and more fun.

2-Keep an eye on the side of the road for shiny little green lights. (Deer eyes)

3– Use your high beam at all times. Cars are not used to see bikes at 2:00 AM.

4– Keep your visor and windshield clean. It pays to see!!!

5– Keep your distance from cars and other riders.

6– Dress accordingly. Be seen! It is ok to look like a neon sign!

7– Enjoy the peace and quiet for it is what makes night riding what it is. Peaceful

Glossary

Poutine: An artery clogging mix of best damn French fries on earth, Caillette Cheese (Some have the audacity to call them cheese curds) and gravy together served in a deep bowl.

Pucker factor scale: The scale on which the contraction of the sphincter muscle is measured after a rather tense (Freaky) moment. Ranging from 1 to 10. 1 being when you can feel your innards (In my case, testicles too) contract as you realize what mess you are in. 10 being where your sphincter has no longer to ability to keep what should stay in from coming out.

Pucker factor: The seriousness at which one goes through the pucker factor scale. It is a physical and a psychological feeling which is also often translated into a sudden violent combination of swears and leather mound creating muscular convulsions.

Teflon underwear: Special underwear or undergarment needed when reaching a pucker factor of 10

Swears: Tabarnac, Colisse, Sincreme, Esti, sacrament, St-Ciboire, soeur blindee, Souffleux de trombone, Calvert, Mule ensoleillée d'apocalypse de crises (Serious stuff) Terms commonly called swears. Profanity is also used in describing these words that are spat out of one's soul's deepest parts. To French Canadian scholars these would be shocking (The hell with them anyway)

Note: Many more are available and can also be custom made, depending on the event.

Leather mound: the little mound or amount of leather or seat covering material that has been sucked up one's ass as he/she progresses from factor 1 to 10 on the pucker factor scale. This little mound of material has been known to remain visible long after the high pucker moment, adding to it a certain level on evident truth...

Frosty: 2007 BMW F650 Dakar motorcycle who has been through Canada in winter in all sorts of conditions that would have demolished anything else. She has witnessed firsthand all the conditions described in the previous page.

She is not retired yet because as of the writing of this book another trip is planned to do it again, but this time to reach Goose Bay Labrador.

Newfoundland Cavalry: Those wonderful people from Newfoundland who have been with me during the whole trip. Planning my arrival, organizing places to stay and also putting in place a network of people who were reporting my position at all time. Some followed me without me ever knowing they were there. They were truly my cavalry who made The Rock what it was.

Holyshitness: Culmination of emotions resulting from the combination of Duhness, Dammitness and sometimes Notsobrilliantness and the realization that the event was not pleasant, and that the outcome could have been catastrophic. This normally ends with a pucker factor that is rather high on the pucker factor scale. They are most often referred to as "I will never do this again!" moments. One's blessings are often referred to, and thankfulness is also often expressed in a cussing and swears filled way. Despite the "Holy" in Holyshitness, there is nothing holly about it and one should refrain from experiencing it around prude people, children and churches.

Duhness: One of the reasons why Holyshitness exists. It consists of a lack of belief in how one self could be so stupid and the inability to understanding why this bad call was made despite the evidence (s) that it would lead to Dammitness. This is one of these moments where one immediately looks around to make sure no one has witnessed this awful mistake. Loss of health (Limbs) and properties in this case is never as important as not losing face or hurting one's ego. This behavior is mainly seen in males.

Dammitness: Closely associated to Duhness, it differs in immediate reactions directly following the said event. While Duhness is mainly felt with a combination of smiles and shrugging, it is also expressed with an "I can be forgiven" or "I can explain this!" Dammitness on the other hand is mostly accompanied by an "I can't F%$#@ believe I did this!" facial expression. The physical evidence of Dammitness is mainly expressed in the form of throwing things around. Cussing, kicking of the ground and bad communication with the people who are witnessing it all.

Notsobrilliantness: This a rare occurrence but nevertheless widely experienced. The differences between Notsobrilliantness and its closest cousins Duhness and Dammitness are subtle. It is in the "Final" results that it differs. If the result is not or cannot be associated with blood, maimed people, loss of properties and material destruction but there is evidence that one cannot explain why it turned out ok after all, Notsobrilliantness occurred. Luck is at play here and often underestimated. In the case of the male (Where Notsobrilliantness is more powerful) it is mostly ignored as the mind is too busy justifying his action.

Not all your dog barking: A point where it is obvious that even the 2 brain cells you proclaim having have not punched in and come to work. This can be the cause and the source of most words in this glossary. The actual moments of Duhness are accompanied by an empty look and drool coming out of one's mouth. This can be in certain cases a sure sign that life as it was enjoyed could very well be on its last leg.

Caution: when this is observed it is advised to call EMT's and even police to prevent one from injuring his or herself, even though the person at risk obviously doesn't give a crap about safety anymore.

Brass Monkey: Brass Monkey. What part of Brass monkey can't you understand?